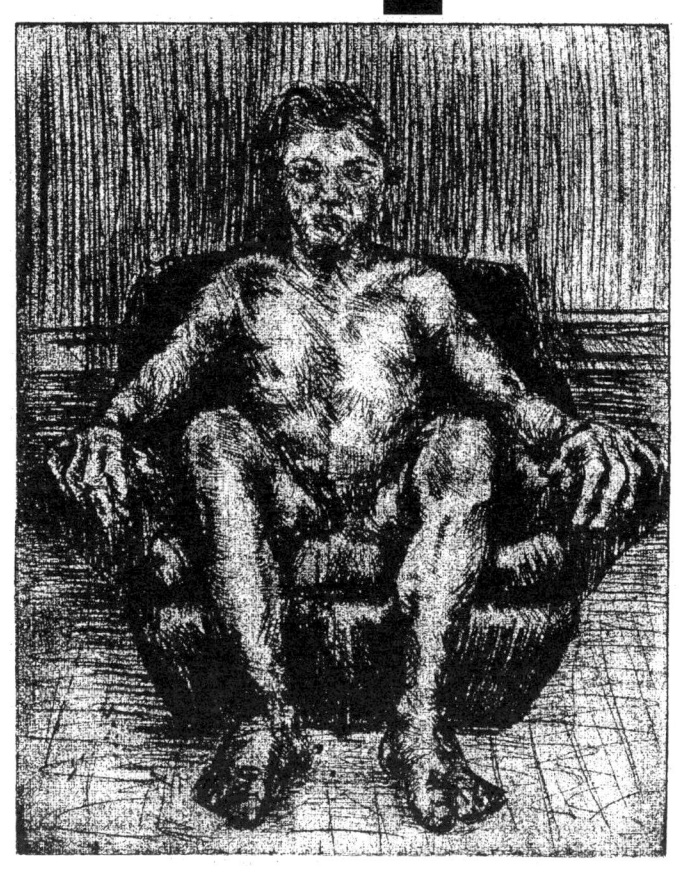

**WRECKING BALL PRESS
HULL • ISSUE 2**

the reater

EDITOR
SHANE RHODES

DESIGN & TYPESETTING
OWEN BENWELL

TYPESETTING
CLAIRE HUTCHINGS & FIONA ARNOTT

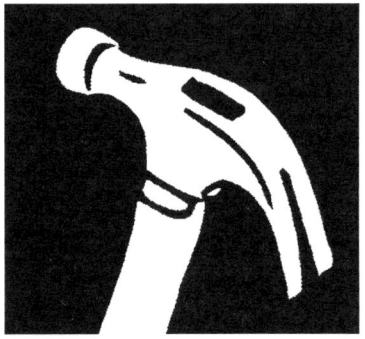

Foreword by SHANE RHODES
Cover Illustrations by OWEN BENWELL

with special thanks to: Russel Jones & Jules Smith

©*All Copyright remains with the artists & contributors.*
Unless for the purposes of review or drunken recitation do not attempt to reproduce any part of this periodical.

All submissions, subscriptions,
and any other material should be sent to :

The Reater
18 Church Street
North Cave
Brough
East Yorkshire
HU15 2LW

PUBLISHED IN 1998 by WRECKING BALL PRESS

THIS EDITION OF THE REATER HAS BEEN PAID FOR BY THE EDITOR

FOREWORD

The shadow of a moth flicks the page I'm reading. I look up to the white blindness of a tired yellow bulb hanging heavy with temporary heat. My eyes recoil, staining the page with silverfish jizz. After blinking a couple of times, I push the button, raise the knib and I'm back to this....

table of contents

devreaux baker
- red wine makes me mean..................13
- marilyn..................14
- runaway..................15
- sleeping dogs and dancing monkeys..................16

andrew parker
- the solution..................21

(illustration **by kevin rudeforth**)

p.d. oliver
- words for use in H.M.P. armley..................27

maurice rutherford
- santos to santa cruz della sierra with lisa st. aubin de terán, 2.1.'97..................31

rosemary palmeira
- hook..................35
- the anchor..................36
- breakthrough..................38

joan jobe smith
- vodka, vaginas, and vomit..................43
- bukowski's book about women..................44
- life's one big rotten tooth and when it's extracted you can't chew anymore..................45
- in the shadow of blood and angels..................46
- beercan in the garden..................47
- feeding my brain on bukowski..................48
- L.A. luv..................49
- leitmotif of our love..................50
- eggs overeasy..................51
- bukowski in beetleland..................52

t. anders carson
- right to release..................57
- sift into the eve..................58

matthew firth
betsy in a bag............(short story)...............................63

jacqueline karp-gendre
august...69
home entertainment..70

(illustration **by kevin rudeforth**)

ian parks
a valley affair..77
enclosures...79
navigation road..80

brian docherty
round up the usual suspects...85
on first looking into the l.l. bean catalogue................86
the artist's mother as simple catholic peasant............88

fred voss
36 years and a million millenia old..........................93
blue skies outside high windows................................94
my fan..95
something they will never get rid of........................96
scholarly dissertation..97
like the air we breath...98
as real as a trainload of steel......................................99
still alive...100
tougher than the steel they cut.................................101
a dream that feeds 10,000 days.................................102
dickwads..103
adrenalin is their middle name.................................104
spice..105
nuts and bolts and donuts...106
paying the price..107
30 year runs..108
grateful...109
it all works..110

peter knaggs
suckers..115
neighbourhood watch...116

(illustration **by kevin rudeforth**)

dean wilson
adidas..123
come what may..124
graham..125

jules smith
poets night on the ss manxman..........................129

linda k.
homage to saint jude...145
inland..146

seamus curran
sea woman..151
taxi ride..152
good friday...154
ashes..155
false spring..156
to lisa..158
stones..160
language lessons...161

peter didsbury
cemetery clearance..165

joanne pearson
message to a friend"*..169

(illustration **by kevin rudeforth**)

charles bukowski
cheer up..175
pain like an old black and white snapshot.........176
that's where they came from..............................177
regrets of a sort..178
darlings of the word...181

norman jackson
feeding the birds..187

andy fletcher
fifteen..........191

(illustration **by kevin rudeforth**)

geoff stevens
personally defaced by joe orton..........197

gerald locklin
bud powell on verve..........201
this guy and i are..........202
easier than swimming laps..........203
depressing books..........204
the pendulum swings off it's hinge..........205
he leads by example..........206
john james audubon: whooping crane..........208
vishnu, siem reap, 9th century..........209
the riots..........(short story)..........210

labi siffre
workshop..........217
inadequate pronouns..........218
don't worry baby..........219
affirmation..........220

carol coiffait
i guess it's been a long time since
i held my mothers hand..........225
brave..........226
hide and seek..........227
his voice and flesh are gone
or it's a long way to wakefield..........228
photographic evidence..........229

(illustration **by kevin rudeforth**)

reviews..........235

devreaux baker
Mendocino, USA

Red Wine Makes Me Mean

1.
Red Wine makes me mean
not like I can do
anything about it but there the fuck
it is and what in the hell
are you going to do about that?
2.
The last time one of the boys
did his fucking bad ass thing with my daughter
she turns right around and goes "Suck my dick"
God that was good to hear
not like the dead nights
and in between places that
sneak up on you in the dark
and whack you on the back of your skull
so's you can't think straight
it was plain as day and the boys
left her to fuck alone after that bit
I'm here to tell
you.
3.
twenty six no maybe twenty eight stars out tonight
and the cold moon going round and round wiping up
after all the guests are done and gone.
4.
I'm sick to death of all these
fucking white boys who
want to get down and try so hard
to do the walk and all that shit but
what it all comes down to
is what my friend Jack said about
when you got a place to sleep at night
and the cops are leaving you alone
and the sky is your friend
I mean is warmly reaching out
to touch your hair
your face
your mouth and you can taste life
thats what its all about and all
every bit of that other shit
doesn't matter for nothing
god I was proud of my girl.

Marilyn

The winter that closed the coat hanger factory
left sheets of ice hanging off our back porch
the smell of aluminum carried on the wind
followed the workers' bodies like silver wishes
swimming across the Rio Grande.

Late night T.V. convinced our next door neighbor
she really could be Marilyn Monroe,
stuck with a husband out of work
and buzzing on the black and white features
that whispered the words
Happy Birthday Mr. President..

Days her man left town, she practiced kissing herself
in the bathroom mirror,
before crossing the street to stand,
skirt blooming with shadows and wind
in our backyard.

The way she could pirouette herself
into believing songs about diamonds
being a girl's best friend dared us into believing
Marilyn had returned from the dead
and was dancing and singing at our backdoor

until her husband Paul returned
with the taste of whiskey he passed
from his mouth into hers
and carried her home again.

And we were left with the after taste of the dead
dreaming its dream, spinning its impossible story
into a shape we could believe in
dancing that winter in our backyard.

Runaway

First it was this way
there was a secret place you went to swim
alone and naked your body a question mark
dangling in cold blue
you left behind your mothers voice
bleeding through the walls of your room
making you afraid to stay
once you tried hiding beneath the house
counting the feet that swung down the steps
in front of your face
features squeezed shut caked with dirt
nights you warded off sleep
planning your next escape
run away at dawn
cross Albers field
hide out in ditches
get stuck beneath blackberry vines
hear you fathers voice trailing like lightening just behind
stay gone for weeks
sleep in the street
sleep in the bus station
feel the bums fingers slide up your leg
feel his tongue, his breath get stuck in your hair
drink wine with the crazy woman
who lives in the shack next door
have dog dreams,
the way they jump on top of your chest
the way they chase you out of sleep
right back to your home agin
where no one even knew
you had ever gone.

Sleeping Dogs and Dancing Monkeys

Evenings we drive the curving road to the last house
through the winter air one yellow light
wavers in freezing cold
ice coats all the trees
into a dream of summer where our father sits
praying to a liquid saint he clutches
in a small amber glass.
He is reading in brief twilight
while hills fade into
the language of birds, ravens and crackles
drifting down
mantling the whole thing in feathered dark.
He has studied the features
of the man in the moon
read each pitted line
the unforgiving frown
of that small golden mouth
transforming its misunderstood
shape into something familiar as the palm of his hand
wrapped around his favorite whiskey glass.
Out of the winter air a season is lifted
from out of our past
tissue thin flattening its length
right out in front of us
to hell with shadows on the grass
this thing has dimension
this thing can sing
does a little jig on the frosty green
its got a face like a shape shifter
first there's my brother and then its me
and we're blending into one crazy swirl
that has arms and legs and when my father yells
we just dance faster
hoping to please
hoping to make him laugh
funny isn't it how we look like
little monkeys
pirouetting in front of him
the sight of us pulled out of sleep

and stitched like this to the bright side of the world
conjures a taste like copper pennies
causing me to kick dogs awake
until they come running
barking the word fear
so memory inscribes
itself in the darkest reaches of our being
then bursts out when we least expect it
like a barking dog
or a dancing monkey
until the word becomes flesh
and the story is resurrected again and again
in the body
my father sits now
pulling memory like a winter sled
across the edges of his life
while I sit
tasting each word
in the dark.

andrew parker
Liverpool, England

The Solution

Tonight, the Tomahawks
will fly
through a sanguine
Mesopotamian sky
through a lack
of talks.

"We have a firing solution, Sir"
and its running,
cutting it's route
through holy air,
Fire and Forget,
the General is crying
tears of pure regret
as tonight,
the Tomahawks are flying

p. d. oliver

Leeds, England

Words For Use In H.M.P. Armley

FENCE, NONCE, SCREW, PONCE
SKIN, LIGHT, SLOP, FIGHT
COLD, CRAVE, DIG, RAVE
NIXED, FIXED, SHOT, MIXED.

HEAD, GONE, NERVE, TIGHT
BEER, BREW, TIME, FLEW
LIFE, KNIFE, NAUGHTY WIFE
PUKE, SHIT, PISS, LIT.

JUDGE, PRICK, BRIEF, DICK
STRETCH, TWOK, CHASE, LOCK
SMOKE, SPLIT, EAT, BIT
VISIT, PAIN, (DEAR) JOHN, AGAIN.

BLOCK, CUFF, RING, BUTT
HIT, ROCK, BLACK, FLIT
BIRD, HIGH, SQUAT, FLY
RIP, BURN, BLEED, BLAG.

IN, OUT, ON, NOWT
WHIZZ, HACK, LUCK, CRACK
BROWN, CROWN, GOIN', DOWN
SHIRT IN, TONGUE OUT.

GRASS, CUT, GREEN, GUT
PAD, JUMP, JACK THE LAD
WAIT, COUNT, HATE, MOUNT
ARMS UP, HEAD DOWN.

CASE, FACE, WING, RACE
RUN, JUMP, LIE, THUMP
ACHE, CRAMP, RATTLE, DUMP...

maurice rutherford
Bridlington, England

Santos to Santa Cruz della Sierra with Lisa St. Aubin de Terán, 2.1.'97

Soon after changing trains I must have slept;
Lisa was chatting to a man in shades
she'd met in Sáo Paulo where the sun
back-lit the arsehole of the world. We'd swept
away from Luz, from crack cocaine, dawn raids,
bent cops, cheap lives, the rule of knife and gun.
I couldn't quite make out their Portuguese
with Villa-Lobos in the background, so
I'd nodded off. The motion of the train?
The heat, her voice, the music? All of these?
I blinked through Campo Grande, its plateau
of sugar-men, heard Lisa's voice again,
crashed out past San José, missed Santa Cruz
completely. Woke to Yorkshire's local news:
the after-Christmas snows, a car-crash scene,
my wife's "A drop more plonk? The dustman's been".

(previously poem of the month, Subtle Flame).

rosemary palmeira
Beverley, England

Hook

Hook that you have in me
thrash and mean me though you might
rage and turmoil me into
white trembling anger
and indignation sleep-robbing
gashes out red but yet

It is that hook
pulling down tight
around the heartbone
the chafe and yank
the hook of you
holds me hard

I cannot leave
nor let leave thus
I turn back, hate-hurting
blind-crying, disembodied
crushed unbearable
dying the suspense of

Find you again,
unyielding yielding
the line so thin is
stretching so the risk
and huge oh!
Immense love again
holds me in tremendous
grip
the hook
slams
into place.

The Anchor

*I remember the pink plastic basket
I took to school after Daddy died.*

There were sunflowers, arums, camellias,
lemons painted blue, the Siamese cat pink.

Teacher showed us the meaning of "nestle"
her jumper of fluffy lemon angora...

Storytime was three entranced faces
Aslan and the Pilgrim are mine forever.

*Blank years; a chrysalis soft and drowsy
spun a white gauze of forgetfulness.*

I remember the sore on his leg after swimming
against rocks, my licking it better.

We climbed over the round orange pantiles
the gardener poured boiling water in the wasps' nests.

I used to sniff "Benzine" from the utility cupboard
and stagger "all dotty" down the garden path.

*I saw white horses, pull an ebony hearse,
heaped with gardenias - How! I wanted to leap.*

We took away giant snails from off the cabbages
they came crawling back, in armies, by night.

Over the wall, was the long knife grass
and bittersweet flowers you could suck and spit out.

I remember my first walk in the night-time
crickets, moon, warm breeze. His hand.

We moved in winter, bare floorboards
iron bedspreads, falling snow.

I remember his tenor in the Sunday drawing room
he sung of storm and an "Anchor that keeps the soul".

He gave me a new sixpence, to fetch his medicine
I had to go all the way down to town alone.

"Honesty ' grows opaque-you have to peel off
the outer skins to reveal the bright pearly disc.

I remember he showed me the wild waves rushing
over the end of the pier, and I wasn't afraid.

Breakthrough

The lights of the city
Are upraised on glass stems
High over the black lurking river
that is glimpsed, never pursued.
The city folds in entices
With importance of options;
On the stone pavement, only
The heaps of leaves, sole
Bird's song breaks
The alabaster edge,
Startles the stretched sheet,
The immaculate thought.

joan jobe smith
Long Beach, USA

Vodka, Vaginas, and Vomit

The first time I ever saw Bukowski
was in 1973 when he read from *Factotum*
on the stage at Cal State U Long Beach
read the pages about the happy
fellatrice bobbing on and off his
pecker and while he grinned and
sucked vodka, the young feminists
in the audience got angrier and
angrier and finally got up and
walked out. I'd worked seven years
as a go-go girl and thought
I'd seen it all and almost had
except for this: a drunken poet
some called genius and young feminists
called a chauvinist s.o.b. pig.
Maybe it was the 12 years gapping
between me and the feminists that
made me understand Bukowski more
than they did, maybe it was my
stupidity, but I fell in love with
him, his audacity, his veracity, his
revelations of women, good, bad, and
ugly, all his women got down on the
page, real or imagined, ravenous
romances, pagan pandemonia of
screwball, screwed-up, wanton, weird,
woebegone women. I wasn't like any
of them. I was staid and ordinary
but I fell in love with him anyway
my way of always falling in love
with men I misconstrue as Heroes:
my first Hero FDR when I was two
who helped perp Pearl Harbour, then at
16 I fell for that high school football
hero who tried to murder me with his
bare hands. Ah, Charles Bukowski,
Knight Errant of the Thornbush of Life:
I was yours, your Guinevere, drawn with
invisible ink, disappearing before you
blinked open your eyes after a long, hard
poetry night of vodka, vaginas, and vomit.

Bukowski's Book About Women

Bukowski called me one night drunk
like he always was after midnight and
he told me he was writing a book all
about women he was calling Women and
maybe he was going to write about me.

Oh, I said flattered he was going to
write about me. What are you going to
write? I asked. Are you going to write
about my nose? After all you never did
give me a copy of the ode you said you wrote
about my nose. And although I've always
had low self esteem, knowing he might
write about me made me feel suddenly cute
so I asked: are you going to write about
how I was the one who got away?

Hell, no, he said, if I write about you at all
it'll be what a bad editor you are and how
you're the only editor in the '70s who
didn't take all the poems I sent you and how
stupid you were.

He was right. He sent me enough poems for
the literary journal I edited for a chapbook
and I sent all back but three because they'd
offended me, had stuff in them about men
pissing and saying fuck a lot. I always regretted
sending back those poems, not doing a
chapbook of those poems. But I never
regretted that Bukowski never wrote
about me in his book about women.

Life's One Big Rotten Tooth And When It's Extracted You Can't Chew Anymore

Bukowski once had a crush on me, maybe, but
that's like saying I once saw a pink sunset. How
many pink sunsets are there in the first place that
makes the one you last saw the most significant?
And Bukowski kissed me, once, as he was leaving
my party I'd given in his honor, the one-millionth
party a little mag editor had given him, and the
worst one, for I'd invited my fellow law students
and some assorted poets. Poetry and jurisprudence:
a living bunch of mixed metaphors and diverse
adversity there'd ever be, and Bukowski said
his usual Wildman things, plus told near-libelous
lawyer jokes, pretended to urinate in a wine bottle
and, worse, pretended to drink it, and the law
students shrivelled in horror and poets took notes
for future Bukowski poems while Linda King
hollered, Bukowski, you're fulla shit. Party vibes
made of barbed wire, Pearl Mesta I was not, Pearl
Harbor more like it, and finally everyone went home,
Bukowski the last to leave because there was beer left
and Linda King wouldn't let him take it into her car
because she didn't want no open-container charge
against her if some red-necked Orange County cop
stopped them so out of a smoky-room dud of a party
Bukowski grabbed me like a grizzly would something
not as fuzzy, he squeezed the breath out of me and
kissed me, and while he murmured Mmmmm, I,
terrified as Linda watched, peed my pants warm all the
way down my faded, patched bellbottom jeans, into
the décolletage of my worn-out Dr. Scholl's wooden clogs.
Ah, memories, memories.

In the Shadow of Blood and Angels

An insomniac and nailbiter, my credo
since the crib has always been:
"If you expect the worst, then when
it doesn't happen, you're happy"
but it didn't work those two years
I tried to worry myself well when
I was a bloody mess with tumours
and became so weak with anaemia
I couldn't turn on tv without hearing
angels sing my name. Cherry-pie-drip
transfusions and sledgehammer surgery
saved my life at the same time Bukowski
got leukemia so I wrote my first letter
to him in 10 years, offered him
my hope for his good health, hope
contrary to my credo to expect the
worst. "Stay tough, "I wrote him,
"kick this leukemia in the butt with
the same German magnum force you did
T.B." and of course he never wrote me
back, not while he carried his bundles
of darkness and he died and I lived
and now everywhere you look there are
angels: angel postage stamps, angel
pins on people's shoulders, angel boxes,
cups and saucers, angel socks and lollipops.
If only one of the angels smoked a cigar
and had pockmarks on his face and would
write down good hard words to tell us
what's been going on since he got his wings.

Beercan in the Garden

After the poetry reading, Bukowski was
supposed to go to a Tea in his honor, yes,
a Tea, and cookies, for Bukowski, sponsored
by the good people of the nearby First
Assimilationist Church, no, no booze, the
good church people probably thinking his
Henry Chinaski persona mere fiction, and
I drove him in my white Volkswagen there
the Laguna Beach aquamarine sky above
the church steeple matching the horizon
high sea, the geraniums and birds of paradise
in full bloom August smiles and wearing their
best party hats and when Bukowski saw all the
good church people standing on the neatly mowed
green-green grass, saw the men in their good
Sunday suits, the women in their whitest frocks,
waiting, watching for The Great Poet's arrival,
Bukowski told me, Don't stop, keep going, I
need a beer, so I drove him to the nearest
liquor store where he bought a 12-pack, snapped
open a can and told me to get the hell outa here
so I drove him to my out-call masseuse girlfriend
Lucy's house in a bad part of Santa Ana and
Bukowski was glad to meet her and her pimp
boyfriend Brucie, shook their hands, flirted with
Lucy, and while she fixed us spaghetti we drank
chianti and then we ate and talked all night
Bukowski making us laugh till 4 in the morning
when Linda, the First Linda, drove him back home
tp L.A., and I didn't see Bukowski again for a year
and the good, tea sipping, cookie - munching good
church people of the First Assimilationist Church
didn't see Bukowski again,
ever.

Feeding My Brain On Bukowski

Bukowski was not impressed with me
when I was accepted for a master of
fine arts degree by the #2- rated
university in America and he told me,
"My main criticism of you, Joan, has
always been that you plugged in
too much to the college scene.
That's a bigger mirage then love.
You should feed your brain on me."
And he wasn't impressed when I told
him that at the university I'd be taught
by famous writer profs and he told me,
"The most vicious people that I have
known, those furtherest away from
reality and compassion are the college
profs.And these teach. Be careful, Joan".
Nor was he impressed when I got a story
accepted by the Paris Review: "Paris
Review? That literary (bleep) bevy of
inbred snobs." Then when I graduated
from grad school, couldn't find a teaching
job, had to work as a proofreader and hung
my MFA degree on the wall for a dartboard
and found out once and for all how
no-good my no-good husband was,
telling this all to Bukowski on the
telephone one night, he told me, "None
of our lives or anybody's life ever quite
makes it. The damnation instead of the
dream appears to win out. Our goddamned
mothers never warned us."Of course, this
did not make me feel better, even when
he said, "you mustn't give up trying."
And I went on with my damnation and
Bukowski went on to the dream.

L.A Luv

Bukowski said to me: "It's true that
I want to fuck you and it's true that
I don't want to fuck you. Fuck ain't
all that hot shit. I want flow. I'm
not that horny that I want to feed you
a line of shit that will lead you
to the end of my cock" and although
it was the '70s of bad boogie nights and
cocaine meringue and loving the one
you're with and people singing that
love was a four - letter word, I'd
expected more gentle into the dark
night from the mellifluous Great Poet.
The '70s decadent decade confused me
while I looked for true love amongst the
ruined haystacks of L.A. that would
soon be crunched by corporate clamp-
claws: married to a no-good husband, my
lover didn't love me, and soon I'd
have a new lover who'd tell me; "Why
should I tell you I love you merely
to validate your existence?" I was
certain in 1977 that there was a
poisonous stardust in the L.A. sky
that sickened everyone and made them say
fuck instead of love. It would take me
12 more years to find my Robert
Browning and had I'd known I'd find
him, it would've made things easier then
to settle for luv. And when Bukowski said
to me that night that "we'll wind up link
sausage on cracked china." it would
not have seemed that the world, that
L.A., were so close to coming to
an end and that the palm trees in the
horizon becoming exclamation
marks and tarantulas the proof of it.

Leitmotif of Our Love

Although liking Bukowski's poetry
was one of the things that brought
my poet husband and me together, one
of the Leitmotifs of Our Love, we
are having a fight about Bukowski
started when I called Bukowski
a spoiled brat.

What do you mean? asks my poet husband,
then says, His father beat the shit out
of him all the time.

Yeah, for not minding him, not mowing
the lawn right, getting drunk, staying out late.

What do you mean? Bukowski grew up
in the Depression.He suffered.

He grew up in the Garden of Eden of L.A.
He didn't go cold and hungry like my
Texas Dust Bowl folks did, he didn't
have to pick cotton like my father did
And Bukowski was a draft dodger too.

What do you mean? Bukowski was protesting
a war he didn't believe in, a conscientious objector.

He was a coward, I say, the mother of his
only child was a WAC in World War 2,
she has twice the balls Bukowski had.
And he's a misogynist, too, and a misanthrope.
And a compulsive gambler and a brute, he
kicked poor pretty little Linda Lee Beighle
out of her chair in that Barbet Schroeder tape
and a lot of Bukowski's poetry is vulgar.
You're really in a bad mood today, aren't you?

Yes, I am, I say then he says, Let's change the
subject then, to something less controversial
like maybe Adolph Hitler.

Eggs Overeasy

I was frying eggs overeasy when
I heard Bukowski had died and
suddenly the yolks came alive,
grew to the size of heavyweight
Golden Gloves smashing my spatula
and jaw while the kitchen swelled
shut around me like a big, blackened
eye. His obituary was in the Thursday
newspaper, my favourite paper of the
week for the Food Section, the recipes
(this week sickening ones of what to
do with peanuts), the supermarket ads
(this week St. Pat's Day specials,
corned beef for 89 cents a pound,
cabbage for nine, rye $1.69 he'll
never eat again, if he ever did,
or the wine I later drink with my
husband who mourns more than me
as he listens to a Bukowski Live tape
and reads over and over the only letter
Hank ever wrote him. Hank never knowing,
too busy to care, that his life changed
ours, that we'd come to know his mojo
poetry as well as the backs of our hearts
where manna and mortality are inscribed.
We'd wanted him to live to be 400,
after all, he was 200 at 30, he was
supposed to keep telling it like it is
forever, our Poet Man, nexus and
code breaker of nether worlds. But
no one ever dies when you want
him or her to, death seldom an Ides
of March or hemlock time for which
you can set your alarm clock as, as he
was quoted in his obituary, you carry in
one hand a bundle of darkness that
accumulates each day. The eggs
overeasy were the coldest I ever ate,
a March ninth wind blowing in through
the window turning them to ice).

Bukowski in Beatleland

In Beatleland, at the Everyman Theatre
bistro in Liverpool, after I read a poem
about Bukowski, a 30something feminist
comes up to me and asks me about
Bukowski, asks how I can like that man
when he was such a woman hater.
She's lusty and gutsy, a pretty woman,
a cross between Bukowski's Frances Dean
Smith and Linda King and instead of
doing my Apologia for Bukowski like I
usually do for young women Bukowski
haters, I tell her Bukowski would've
really liked her and she smiles and
asks, He would've? Yes, I say, he
would've really liked your guts and
beauty. And we stop talking about Bukowski
and start talking about *my* poetry.

t. anders. carson
Portland, Ontario, Canada

Right to release

I encrust my wounds
into the wife
of a German priest.
She's afraid of my stories
of my unrelenting brother.
The way his travail
incorporates mudslinging
with the cops,
periodic break and enters
and fooled drug scandals.
The lonely cowboy
is tired of holding
a molotov cocktail.
At any time that phone
rings,
I explode into a frenetic
tizzy.
His friend that kindly
knocked out two of his teeth,
for respect's sake,
was slaughtered 3 months
ago.
Police wanted to say
suicide but it is difficult
for both father and son
to swallow one bullet
at nape of neck.
Let's check.
The murderer is still
on the noose
I hope when they nab him
they won't bust loose
as our old L.A. friend
the Juice.
Holy cats!
Let's see how long
they last.

Sift into the eve

Wallows of smoke undulate
around my cleavage.
Grime is peeled off my swollen forehead.
The same as a clown's make-up
you can see peeling only
from the first row.
Dig Dig Dig Dig my own shattering grave.
The calls come from Bell.
Your faint whisper of insanity
spirals through my telephone cord.
Your allowance is spent.
Your rent is ceased.
Your school is burned.
You will twitter on the abyss.
Tippy toe over the edge,
with only dental floss holding you
tightly to a stone.
Too bad it is waxed,
it makes for difficult grip.
Sirens fill the air.
Shotguns fold people in half,
as drive by's seep into sleepy
Canadian towns.
First car stereos,
then young offenders' sentences
it is only your children you fear.
So I'll go and try my luck
at the Bingo hall again.

matthew firth
Fife, Scotland

Betsy in a Bag

Lionel paces and stews. Throws his hands up in the air. It's been almost three weeks and still nothing. He leans over the pot and smells the damp earth. Prods the soil with a grubby index finger.

His other plants are doing fine. He knows which ones need a lot of sunlight. He waters them all regularly. Dusts the leaves as required. One cactus he's had six years. In the same pot.

Frustrated, he storms into the kitchen. He removes the instructions from under a pink and green fridge magnet shaped like a daisy.

BETSY IN A BAG it reads across the top.

Under that: **Take Her Out and Get Instant Results! Instant Satisfaction!**

He drops his eyes to the instructions:
- bury seeds 6-8 centimetres beneath the surface in a medium sized pot
- water moderately every-other-day for ten days
- place water pot in shaded area
- do not place pot directly in front of window
- harvest after ten days

Lionel reads the instructions twice, making sure he didn't miss anything.

"I followed it to the letter," he mumbles, dropping the flyer on the linoleum.

Back in the living room, Lionel settles in a wicker chair. Betsy's pot sits alone in the centre of a small table across the room.

"It'll grow, "he whispers. "It has to."

He stares at the solitary clay pot.

He stands and walks towards it.

"Betsy," he coos. "Come on dear. I won't bite."

He leans close, running his callused hands around the base of the pot, stroking it.

"We could be happy together."

He leans closer still, pressing his lips into the cool soil, urging Betsy to show herself. He nudges the lip of the pot with his nose playfully.

"Betsy dear? Betsy dear? Come out, come out, where ever you are."

He drops his left hand down below the table into his shorts. His right hand holds the pot firmly.

"Come on love. Come on love," Lionel chugs through clenched teeth, the table shaking slightly, Betsy rocking in her pot.

"I paid good money for you," he says a minute later, the soothing tone of his voice replaced by a deeper, more guttural drawl.

Finally, his face flushed, Lionel spits, "MAYBE THIS WILL HELP YOU GROW," while tipping the pot toward him, pressing it against his stomach.

Twenty minutes later, his morning shower complete, Lionel walks back into the living room. He looks over at Betsy. He's not wearing any glasses, but, through a squint, he's positive he can see a small shoot winking over the edge of the pot.

"That a girl Betsy," Lional says, scratching his chin. "That a girl."

jacqueline karp-gendre
Vaux sur Mer, France

August

They're standing six to seven deep
at Gégé's fruit and veggie stall,
elbowing for apricots artichokes
cut-price peaches *brugnons*
Charentais melons *"pour manger à midi"*

while Madame Patry has been up
since eight basting her BBQ
poulets au grain and the paella girl
shovels great mounds of fried prawns
chicken drum sticks saffron rice.

Cars fill the market place with exhausted
drivers and air. Over at the chemist's
an irate tourist gives a young man
a sharp lesson in queueing manners -
but we locals know he's right.

Just up the hill an oldish man parks and
pours out litres of beer-brown piss
in someone's lane, beneath their letter box
- taking his time to shake the last drops off -
the postlady will soon be here and treading in it.

I press down my window and shout
Espèce de cochon! Et les WC place du marché?
We've paid enough in rates
for new loos in the market place
to do without a *vieux pisseux* like you!"

Home entertainment

Lunch is a silent affair. A few frenzied questions -
Have you phoned? Was there any post?
Did that booking come through from AB Voyages?
Then we concentrate. Important matters.
Scraping up yogurt. Spitting cherry pips.
Wondering who will make the coffee.
Watching grim accidents. You chew, ear tilted
towards the voice, eyes on the disasters.
Do I need an A/D converter to get digital with you?
Is it my analogue face you reject?
Or is pay-to-view football your latest whim?
I am on near-demand you know, and half the price.

ian parks
Mexborough, England

A Valley Affair

A silent girl with auburn hair
moved in the cottage opposite.

Between us there was nothing
but the valley's steep incline;

the window where she used to sit
as winter turned to spring.

She lived in rumours heard
around the town: a broken marriage,

bruises, kids; a midnight
crossing then the trek

along that wild peninsula
to here - a slate-and-granite cottage

with a sloping roof,
blocking the tangled entrance

to a disused copper mine.
At night a single candle

drew my gaze, turning
her body over in my dreams.

I knew we shared a birth-sign
when she came, asking for water

at a neighbour's farm
and watched her white legs flexing

as she started up the hill,
a transparent plastic canister

slung over one bare arm,
needing both to help and look

as if each impulse were the same.
What made me hesitate?

But hesitate I did - until
the year's first crocus

nudged the soil. Then I was up
and running, making for

that crumbling cottage
and its drystone wall - and found

what you expected me to find:
cold ash flaking on the grate,

a rolling bottle, mattress, rugs;
an absent presence

filling out the place. The latch
still ticking on her gate.

Enclosures

Outside, the paid-up world begins to freeze
its assets which are valueless.
But here you lie secure, at ease
with love and what we make of it.

After a day in which the quality of light
dictated everything we did
we let the candle drip itself a shape
around the empty bottle at our feet.

Drystone walls enclose us. The fells
are weighted down with powerlines.
And someone somewhere claimed the right
to parcel up the darkness where we sleep,

as if the common ground could take
the sealed impression of his signature.
We wake to fresh lucidities.
The frosted window sprouts its new designs.

Navigation Road

An unexpected halt:
and part of me
was five miles down the track,
lost in the thought
of how it felt
to wake up in your arms.
Pale sunlight seeped across
the slanting roofs
of another undistinguished
northern town - red brick,
forgettable - that only
made it to the map
because the lines converge.
Mist cleared from the canal.
A schoolgirl boarded, dropped her book,
and left it where it fell.
From now expect
a slight shift of the heart.
Our hands are linked
under these winter sheets;
our tracks are running parallel.

brian docherty
London, England

Round up the usual suspects

The Hornsey Journal has a column called 'Crime Shorts'.
No, it's not a modern version of the striped jersey,
the sack stencilled SWAG. A list of those caught
in or after the act. Sundry neds, villains, psychos.

This week's haul has Gerry Conlon, Paddy Armstrong.
Couldn't wait, could they? Bailed for possession
of cocaine and Ecstasy. Perhaps they got the habit
inside. Or they're that sort anyway. Take your pick.

Funny isn't it. They get out, do something silly.
Remember George Davis, the campaign to free him?
He couldn't wait either. Caught in the act
with a shooter at the Allied Irish Bank. Old habits.

Everyone is equal in the blind angel's theatre.
Stick a sawed-off in a bank clerk's face,
stick a coke-filled bank-note up your nose,
the law proclaims you equally guilty. 14 years.

The man in the mutton-chop whiskers, the wig,
the 18th century mind, has the power to throw
away the key to your future. A menace to society.
Thrust back into the belly of the beast.

You have no right to the rest of your life.
It is harder then ever to avoid the authorities.
The hyenas will camp outside your door
whether you are logged in Largs or Tufnell Park.

Writing books is not a good idea. Live quietly,
take a menial job. If you go to the pictures
a voice will call you up later. "We will rape
your corpse & eat the evidence." Be a good boy.

On First Looking into the L.L.Bean Catalogue

I find out several things I always wanted to know,
like the importance of layering your clothes
in the Maine winter and that the prices are
surprisingly reasonable, in fact by middle class
American standards must be downright cheap.
I think of Robert Lowell telling us via
Jonathan Raban's Introduction to his <u>Selection</u>.
"My immediate family, if you have an English equivalent,
would be the Duke of Something's sixth cousins",
then being told by someone who knew him at Essex
that Lowell had no need to work for money.
"Oh yes, he had all the Trust Funds",
and indeed Lowell deploys all the names
of the families who own and operate Boston
as his familiar relatives, and writes cosily
of Nautilus Island as one of the family homes,
condescends to 'our summer millionaire
who seemed to leap from the pages of an L.L Bean
catalogue'. I imagine this character
like Jay Gatsby, ordering bales of shirts
but never quite shedding his dubious past.
Most of the catalogue models smirk to camera
as if the photographer has been telling them
dirty jokes to keep their minds off the cold,
or they usually do their bit in more downmarket
doorstops, and this is a welcome vacation,
knowing as they pretend to saw logs, ski,
pull sledges, read books or eat flapjacks,
they will be scrutinised by the socially acceptable.
Perhaps they even have a secret history
of Adult Lingerie catalogues or skinflicks.
Here the silk underwear is laid out flat and empty
and for some reason I think of those mailorder tomes
with their glossy pages of bras, knickers,
corsets, Y-Fronts, all filled to perfection,
then the pornographic story I found in a mag
while I was waiting for a Medical once,
where a man with the 'enormous tool'
had nothing on except his Union Suit and

'she started to climax before he was fully inside her'
then several pages of shop till you drop.
I assumed from the bad pun a Union Suit
was that sort of blue one piece overall
worn by calender connoisseurs in garages
but L.L.Bean's underwear looks like longjohns.
I am reminded of a film I saw years ago,
<u>The Missouri Breaks</u>, with Marlon Brando
toting a ridiculous Irish accent and a long rifle,
where he hams it up so badly he deserves
to get his throat cut by Jack Nicholson,
but the point dear readers, is that Brando
or at least his character, a bounty hunter,
shot a minor character from a quarter of a mile
through a toilet door and his victim staggered out
in his Union Suit spurting blood onto the snow,
and that it might have been one of the very few
Westerns where it is snowing during the action
and we all felt for this character who had to trudge
to the jakes and get his kit off then be shot,
but now I am relieved to find that a Union Suit
has, according to p.81, 'one piece convenience
in outdoor conditions' with a 'full buttoning
seat in back' for only $63.50 (Men and Women)
or $67.00 Tall and Extended Size (Men Only)
and I learn that the colours are gender divided,
both can wear Red but Light Grey is Men only,
Rose Floral is reserved for Women, who can be
Off White or Periwinkle in Tops and Bottoms.
This will save confusion on dark winter mornings
and offers the option of separatist or bisexual codings.
No doubt bars favoured by staff of the Maine
Department of Inland Fisheries and Wildlife
echo nightly to jokes along the lines of
"It's not the bear and it's not the Pope
but L.L.Bean customers who shit in the woods".

The Artist's Mother As Simple Catholic Peasant

My Andrei was a good boy.
The mask he wore for you
was just that, all thought
there was nothing behind it
like he was a robot.

Well he was, he worked
at his movies, his art,
but underneath all that
Manhattan varnish he was
still my son, still a good
Catholic who came to visit
his mother regular.

          Oh you
didn't know that did you,
you think New York is the
whole world, outside is
a wilderness. Well I tell
you my father God rest him,
came from Ruthenia, from
real forest with real wolves.

So my Andrei painted your
America for you, your Monroe,
your Presley, those soup cans.
Real life - eating soup
in front of a television.

I taught him his Catechism.
He was an altar boy till
he was 14 then he chose Art.
I wanted a priest in family
but I did not stand in his way.
This interview - 15 minutes you say?

fred voss
Long Beach, USA

36 YEARS AND A MILLION MILLENIA OLD

The poet was
an old steel ladder 200 feet up in the cold sea air
on the roof of an old hotel 3 blocks away,
he was
a puddle of rainwater evaporating in an alley behind 6th Street
and an old Volvo
abandoned in an alley and a pool cue
in a rack somewhere downtown with chalk all over its tip,
he didn't move for an hour in that chair on his porch
and he was Buddah
under the yew tree
and a 3,000-year-old thimble
and the top branch of a 2,000-year-old redwood
waving in the sun
and all the love
in the letter of a soldier to his wife before he charged
out of a WW1 trench into battle,
and when he died
under a tree sitting like a man playing chess
or in tune with the furthest fingertip of the universe
the poet was
the newborn babe
so innocently opening its eyes
for the first time.

BLUE SKIES OUTSIDE HIGH WINDOWS

In the shadow
of 50-foot-high vertical bedmills
spewing out clouds of oil and coolant that stink
like insecticide mixed with gasoline,
in the shadow
of the green sides of machines that tower over us
and take the best
of our strength and endurance and spirit
as we spend our lifetimes turning out parts,
in the shadow
of young laughing men
turned into old men with trembling jaws
and lines of anger carved into their faces as if with a knife,
in the shadow
of 20 or 30 years in a cage with tin walls
where men taunt and torment and scream at
each other until apes
look good,
in the shadow
of harder-than-rock machines with 1/4-ton gears
and all the men dead
who had no choice
but to work away their lives
on them,
we keep our eyes
on the light in blue skies outside high windows
anyway.

MY FAN

My Lead Man
had seen my book GOODSTONE when he was over
in building 79
and he came up to me at my machine
and looked at me with glowing eyes and said,
"Yeah, I saw it it's blue and it has that picture of you on the back!
It's this size—-"
He held his hands up parallel to the floor and then perpendicular,
framing GOODSTONE'S $5 \, 1/2$ x $8 \, 1/2$' size as if it were a piece of aluminum
to be cut into an aircraft part.
"Yeah I saw your book of poems, poet!"

I shot a concerned look at him.
"Just don't show it to Hugh Wrighttower," I said, invoking the name
of the Goodstone Aircraft Company president.

"Oh don't worry!" my Lead Man shot back.
"If he saw it, he'd want to meet the poet, and then he'd come out
here and I'd point you out and he'd see the way you look and he'd
NEVER believe YOU could be a poet!"

As long as I work in a machine shop I'll never have to worry
about getting a big ego.

SOMETHING THEY WILL NEVER GET RID OF

There is a stench
of oil and coolant and grime years old
suddenly released
when a locknut is cracked loose and cutter and spacers are slid
off an old arbor,
a stench reeking
of something on the blackened concrete floors and in the corners
of old cabinet drawers full of bolts
covered in old rotting machine grease
and the very air
of the machine shop that turns the insides of a man's nostrils
sour
and settles on his skin,
a stench
belched and spewed out of 30-foot-tall rolling
vertical mills in clouds
of hot smoking oil and coolant and splinters and bits
of cut aluminum or steel that shower
down
all over the machine shop
for 10 or 20 years
on men
who carry it home on their arms and hands and necks
and faces and heads
and wash and wash and wash
but never quite get rid of it,
that last
little trace of the machine shop still always on their skin
and deep
in their souls.

SCHOLARLY DISSERTATION

Curly
comes over from his machine to mine
with the sports section he has been reading while his machine runs
and opens the section to a column of ads
and sticks them in my face and points at them.
"You ever noticed, Fred, how on this page there's always these ads
together—first, you got your 'Penile Enlargement' ad, then,
your 'Hair Replacement' ad —and then you got these ads for the
topless bars and the nude strip clubs!"
Curly slapped the ads on the page with two fingers
and slammed the sports page shut
and began grinning.
"Yep, I think I'll go get a penile enlargement, then I'll go to
the hair replacement clinic— and then, I'll go down to the topless
bar or the strip club and be able to pick up on the foxiest dancer
in the whole place!"

Not even a professor with Ph.D.s in anthropology and sociology
and psychology
could have put a whole culture into a nutshell
better.

LIKE THE AIR WE BREATHE

Loneliness
of the last person on a barstool in a bar at 1 a.m. Saturday night
loneliness
in the rain
dripping off the fenders around cats nestled under cars
loneliness
in the streets so wide and straight for cars to race down
across America
and in all the old people weeping abandoned in wheelchairs
in American convalescent homes wishing
they had been born butterflies
or rats rather than people loneliness
in all the steel bars of all the prisons
and in all the 20 dollar bills
in all the wallets of all the men and women who have worked
40 or 50 hours again on machines
punching out keys or gaskets or earth mover
teeth loneliness
in every shadow in every corner of every diner
in every American city and in all
the bright bright commercials flickering on all our tvs as all
the young women
are finding out that the love in movies doesn't really exist
and all the young black men
are finding out that equality is just a word on a chalkboard
in an expensive college loneliness
in all the broken people begging for love at the foot
of iron Jesuses on iron crosses
in our churches.

AS REAL AS A TRAINLOAD OF STEEL

I don't want to read the critical essays
explaining
Beethoven's music,
or know how much refinement his bust on a mantlepiece
might add to a room,
I want to feel
the crashes of power in his music
the way a man shoving a 20-foot bar of steel
into a blast furnace for the 12th time
in a day feels the heaviness of the steel
in his shoulder and the stink of its filthy burning skin
in his nostril,
I want
the tenderness of love in a trembling violin string
like something in the eye of a steelworker
working 70 hours a week
under the eye of a vicious foreman
at a heart-quaking nerve-shredding 2-ton drop hammer
to put food in the mouth of his child,
I want
the power exploding out of a Beethoven crescendo
like the raw force in the fists of the man digging his bootheels
into a concrete floor
hammering a 1/4-ton steel shank across a machine table
like an animal.
I don't want to learn to understand in University classrooms
exactly what techniques Beethoven used.
I want his music to surge
through me the way the blood surges
through the veins of a man who has
cut steel with the roaring blue flame of a torch
all his life,
I want a Beethoven
as real as the rivers of sweat on the skin
and the leaping of the heart
of a man who must feed a machine 100-pound jackhammer casings all day
to keep his family alive.

STILL ALIVE

This <u>Crucifix in a Deathhand</u> by Bukowski
that I have purchased
for $1,200
is in perfect mint condition
32 years after the summer it was published,
and though I love
the beautiful hand-printed letterpress words
so black and clearly stamped into the beautiful spotless paper
and the gorgeous artwork
and adorning colored artistic paper,
I will still
read it with a frothy beer in my hand
slightly stained with machine grease from the machine shop
where I am grinding away my life
and on its pages
here and there
let fall
a drop or 2 of the beer
and leave
a machine-grease-and-sweat-stained fingerprint
or 2,
to prove
that there is still a man trapped and sweating and struggling to survive
in this world
who in the wonder of the excitement of the genius still so alive
on these pages
leaves a trace of his life
on them.

TOUGHER THAN THE STEEL THEY CUT

The blast furnaces
broke thermometers 20 feet away and burned
the hair off the arms and faces of the steelworkers
and the steelworkers
threw taunts and jeers in each other's faces all day,
the steel mill
hammered the steelworkers' legs with its concrete floor
and pounded their bodies until their hearts skipped
and their jaws shook and they
tormented each other with stares that would kill
if they could,
the foremen
eyed the steelworkers like they were always about to fire them
as they made the steelworkers work
60-hour weeks shoving and wrestling and hammering tons of
steel
until they were asleep on their feet
and the steelworkers goosed each other with broom handles
and pulled each other's beards
and picked mercilessly at each other's weaknesses
until they were trembling on the edge
of murder.
Fire
and machines as big as dinosaurs
pounding and jarring and wrenching their guts out
and gruelling hours that reduced them to jelly
just weren't enough
for men who wanted to be tougher
then the steel they cut.

A DREAM THAT FEEDS 10,000 DAYS

They carry 5-ton loads of steel bars
swinging on the ends of the hooks of 10-ton rolling overhead
cranes
down steel mill aisles
all their lives and don't know why,
they fill up a thousand steel chip bins
with chips of aluminum they have cut
without knowing why as they
lurch and sweat through weeks and years that blur
together,
they beat on vise handles with hammers
until the bones in their wrists and hands
throb all night
and twist and gnarl their fingers
lifting and pressing and shoving
a million pounds of steel
and never for one moment as they grow old know any other
reason why
than the eyes of the foreman who could fire them,
and yet
a thought
of a fish hook
dropped into the sea
or a horse
bet,
come Sunday,
will still light their eyes up with a dream
they can live on.

DICKWADS

Machinists
keep serious deadpan expressions on their faces
as they tell each other to suck each other's cocks
and talk about each other's cocks
being so small they would make good toothpicks
and call each other
useless shit-eating motherfuckers
or ass-wipe son of a bitch dickwads,
standing toe-to-toe and nose-to-nose
with each other
as they stick jaws out at each other
and scream abuse in each other's faces
until
one of the machinists who has had a particularly bad day
or week
begins to fidget and twitch with the unmistakable signs
of uncontrollable
rage
and is a hair's-breadth away from picking up a wrench or hammer,
whereupon
the machinist spewing out the verbal abuse will finally crack
his stone dead-pan face
with the slightest of trembling-with-laughter
it's-only-a-joke smiles
as he takes a couple of steps backward from the other machinist.

Having a great deadpan may be a lot of fun,
but it's not worth dying over.

ADRENALIN IS THEIR MIDDLE NAME

Some machinists
smile whenever a piece of steel cut off by a cutter
on their machine flies
past their ear WHAP into a sheet metal partition
behind their back
or an Allen wrench they forgot to take out of a set screw
in a cutter holder in a machine spindle
shoots across the shop at 100 mph.
They never
wash with soap or put disinfectant
or Band-aid
on a cut,
and when they
slice open a finger on a saw blade
they drip blood across the concrete floor grinning
to the Dispensary and then reappear
to proudly show off
to all the other machinists the big stitches across
the finger.
They suck in as many toxic solvent fumes as they can
and hold down pieces of steel by hand
and drill holes through them with drills in machine head
spindles
that can pick up the pieces of steel
and whirl and throw them like knife blades.
They whistle
while tossing 40-pound blocks of steel with razor-sharp corners
around
in their fingers
over steel machine tables
as managers in offices tremble thinking about it.

"You can't live forever!"
is their favourite saying.

SPICE

He
walks by machinists between machines and throws uppercut punches
that stop an inch before the machinists' bellies
and grins.
He wears boxing gym
and Silver Glove championship and Vegas title fight
T-shirts and runs
up and down the steel stairs in back of the machine shop
in steel-toed boots 10 times
each break
and does whirling kickboxes
at trashcans and challenges
every machinist in the shop to spar with him in the bathroom
at lunch.

The fact that getting in a real fistfight in this machine shop
will result in termination
just seems to add spice
to his delight
in walking around a hair's-breadth away
from one.

NUTS AND BOLTS AND DONUTS

Donuts
are brought in by machinists
in big pink boxes and set on workbenches
on Saturday or Sunday mornings to celebrate
the time and a half or doubletime pay
the machinists are getting for working overtime
and prove
what great good guys they are as they allow
buddy machinists
to dip their hands into the boxes and take donuts at will.
Along with pots of coffee they help
hungover machinists or machinists working that midnight to 7 a.m.
graveyard shift
stay awake and
machinists
who are cracking up or drunk
can stagger around the shop passing them out all night
between trips outside to howl at the moon,
while the holes
in donuts
provide endless fodder for machinist jokes and wisecracks
involving pussies and assholes
and the size of cocks.

Few things in this world are more perfect for machine shops
than donuts.

PAYING THE PRICE

There are the machinists
at 49 or 54 with all their years of Wild Turkey
or Johnny Walker Red whiskey or Popov vodka
drinking
who
come in red-faced and wild-eyed ready to raise their fists at the drop of a hat and laughing
like there couldn't be a wilder more rugged place
for a real man these days to laugh
and raise a fist than the concrete floor
of a machine shop,
who
swagger and bellow outrageous braggadocio all day
with a twinkle in their eye until
the stroke
fells them
in one blow and they walk in white as sheets
dragging a leg
or an arm
to their old workbenches gouged and stained with their lifetimes
of hammering and tool handling and part cutting
to stand
for a week or 2
like monuments to all they were for 30 or 34 years
before the inevitable doctor
who will end all that
and send them home forever
to pay the price for what they were.

30-YEAR RUNS

After years and years under the hundreds of bright flood lights
hanging from the tin ceiling 70 feet above
machinists
wear bright lime
or polka dot suspenders and suck on cigars
or lollipops like they were props
as they polish lines
about how big their cocks are
and the wads they shoot are
and how short the other machinist's cocks are,
perfect
the way they cock a hat on their head
or tap ash off the end of a cigar,
perfect
an indomitable wise-guy smile
or a swagger
or an upturned thumb gesture
or the way they have polished smooth a steel stool
with the seat of their pants for 20 years,
turning into
that guy in the corner on the internal grinder wearing a cowboy hat
who likes to shout, "GRIIIIIIIIND!!" whenever anyone walks by,
or the guy
in matching khaki pants and shirt and hat
who has a twitch in his right eye
and always says, "Well, ready to HIT it?" to everyone he sees at
6:00 a.m. at the start of each workday.
Men
who started out as mere operator at machines
can become characters
in permanent 40-hour-a-week plays
more classic
than any that ever played on Broadway.

GRATEFUL

The homeboy
ex-gangbanger machinists
have their silver glove or black belt championship award
certificates plastered across the outside of their toolboxes
as they spin in the air doing kickboxes at trashcans
and spar in the machine shop bathrooms,
greeting each other at time clocks
doing old fist-knocked-against-fist
palm-rubbing-against-palm
homeboy handshakes,
grinning
with the impossible good luck of now having $20-an-hour jobs
that will save their lives and their families' lives
when once
their lives were on the line in tough-as-hollow-bullet
neighborhoods,
trying
so desperately to learn how not
to go into rage and deadly confrontation over
a nick to a toolbox
or a joke that isn't funny
or one wrong glance too many,
as they make jokes
about blowing each other or supervisors away
with AK-47 assault rifles
and cock their thumbs over forefingers like they were the barrels
of guns
and fire them at each other
and wear
old T-shirts commemorating parties and get-togethers
where dead homeboys are remembered and mourned,
trying
for all they are worth
to wrap their arms around their jobs
and press them to their breasts
and never let them go.

IT ALL WORKS

The crows'
throats work as they caw on telephone wires
and the handle to the old bedmill
works like it slips into gear sending the machine head plunging
toward the machine table,
the black man works the black-knobbed gear shifts
of the forklift sliding the forks under tons of steel bars
to lift them off the train car
and the widower with the bad heart fires up his torch
and cuts through steel bar because it is the last thing in his life
that works.
The raindrops dripping off the pine needles in the mountains
work
and the ant works carrying a piece of leaf 50 times its size
down the sidewalk
and the hands work everytime they interlock their fingers
and the ray of sun works
on the blade of grass,
always
the legs of women are working on men's imaginations
and the oils of Van Gogh
on the soul of whomever looks on them.
Our hearts work.
Whatever set
the seeds of the universe sprouting
works.
The waves work.
Not one has failed for a billion years.
The man
breaking his huge back shoving bars of steel in and out of
furnaces
65 hours a week
to put food in the mouth of his tiny baby son
and the magic that has always been
work.

peter knaggs
York, England

SUCKERS

I remember he eight balled this guy
in Scarborough last winter,

second game, seven balled him in under
two minutes

still he came back, for double
or quits

We don't like people beating us in our....

His palms hit the floor and Ox is at
the Cortina door

as the bottle rolls, I read,
serve chilled.

After expense fifteen quid each
the booty, the loot

The indicator stops its tick, the
baseball bat rolls

and clunks in the boot.

NEIGHBOURHOOD WATCH

Not the smoke from five cremations
that once bounced in a pan on the stove
or the sound of the gas ring whispering
that nursed the potatoes to death.

Not the brother through the snicket
who never got round to a Christmas card
or the woman downstairs
who never spoke to the bachelor next door.

The bloke over the road broke the door down,
caught the milkman swinging the gate,
leaving a pint on boxing day
next to the one, still there.

dean wilson
Hull, England

Adidas

Please don't come on my trainers
they cost me an afternoon
in Earl's Court
with a stand up comedian

and it's best we don't linger
too long here
pigs have a talent
for getting away with murder

We'll be better off
in the elephants graveyard
where the punters are well heeled
and the bar staff turn a blind eye

and come closing
we can wait outside with the other lads
or walk 'round the block
and peer into cars as they slowly pass

Come what may

Your eyes are big and blue
and my aim is true
and the animals went in two by two

So there's nothing to lose
and this isn't a bite
but it might be a bruise

Tread carefully my love
things are starting to hot up
and prevention is better than cure

But remember

Tip-toeing over the dead
won't make much difference
so be prepared for disappointment

It's easy to be wise after the event
and anyway looking back
will get you nowhere
and leave you spent

Oh dear
the best part of a year
has been and gone
and it won't be coming back

So if I want to smell the flowers
in the park I will
and if I want to slim like crazy
and sell what's left

then that's exactly what I'll do

Graham

We are only
four miles from Filey
and I am distantly related
to Dorothy Squires

and your father
played football
in the forties
for Doncaster Rovers

And last night
in Robin Hood's Bay
sat in your car sucking you off
I wanted you to come and never stop

And later on
in bed watching telly
you fell asleep in my arms
and it felt like I belonged

But now
let's go to where Butlins once stood
I went there every year
a long time ago

And when we get back
I'll rake out some photos taken there
of me, my mam and dad
and my little sister

jules smith
Hull, England

Poets' Night On The SS Manxman

PART 1   RSVP

In the Rumoured City, in the old town,
a wine-and-ink sky. The sun is going down
over the river and its coloured lights,
an expanse windy-warm on Summer nights.
A mood is taking over. We will fly
over warehouse rooftops, with Fellini-
vision, "we are sailing, we are sailing..."
towards a painted steamship's stiff rigging.
Magnificent anti-fascist liner,
sharing the 'Rex' in 'Amarcord"s designer,
it is not; it's been tarted-up a treat
by a pub chain, and parked next Humber street.
There are no paying passengers on board,
no Ancient Mariners, nor things untoward,
as yet. No talk in blank verse pentameters
in volumes way beyond water meters,
imbuing testosterone with image,
to part up our unpoetic age.
Until...June 16th, axis of the year,
Spook Night, when zombies dance, as in 'Thriller'.
Swelegantly seedy, history-reeking,
this is the poetic vessel we're seeking.

'The Manxman': fit location
for 3-legged games. A long poem
      on a long night
      on a long boat.
A work of libel and celebration.
A test of invention,
which Keats took to be the Pole Star,
as Fancy is the steam funnel,
and Imagination the rudder,
of poetry.

Now watch batteries fail, paralysing Time.
Warp-factored, promiscuous use of rhyme
causes a White Hole in the temporal,
through the Tidal Surge Barrier's portal.

The wind blows from the Psychic 70s,
reconnecting nutty camaraderies,
Hullensian bacchanals. There's mayhem,
a free period, p.m to a.m.

RSVP, poets and selected guests;
revisit your joint and several quests.
All the figures from the Heroic Page
of Hull Poets. (Or was it the Stone Age?)

From Vaudeville Morgues they are released.
From Crematorium Sports Clubs, deceased
poetes maudits, reconstituted ghosts,
in the mood for dancing, and drinking toasts.

Invitees, decanted from their locals
- The Queens, The Bull, St.John's, The Polar Bear -
arrive. Some saints, scholars, sapphists, yokels,
"a coincidence of talents and atmosphere".

The living look surprised on the gangway.
They were lately in the pub, or in bed.
The dead just manifest themselves, and say
"Before I was rudely interrupted..."

(The Writing Life is a kind of party.
Once you're 'in', it pays to be a smarty,
observing grand entrances and exits,
who's put on weight, who's got the best tits).

The ship's orchestra, it is understood,
is the Hull Phil under Sir Henry Wood,
who play, in good bourgeois middlebrow form,
'Kingston Sketches', then Brahms like a storm.

A Preservation Jazz Band is also on,
to please Larkin, Frank Redpath, Douglas Dunn.
'Dancing on All Decks'. And two fab strippers
are dressed as mermaids, and wave their flippers.

Waiters wearing goblin suits see sense
in satisfying 'the wilder requirements',
so handsome voluptuaries, either sex,
undertake to go down below decks.

For reasons known to himself, and to God,
Pete Didsbury wears a toga. "Daft sod"
the affectionate soubriquet received
as he greets old friends, if I'm to be believed.

"Butter floats in our black tea", he gurgles,
with alcoholic inspiration. "Shit,
Life is a Cabaret, Old Chum. Burgles
the pocket, while you are watching it".

Sean O'Brien, less flaneur than Flann,
is very fond of argumentation
("a pint o' plain is not your only man")
and disputes this with William Mason.

Who turned Quaker, who set out his stalls
after kicking library porters in the balls?
It's Popeye the Sailor Man Flynn,
who's glug-glugging a bottle of gin.
Perverse to his image,
he doesn't like spinach,
and is much preoccupied by sin.

These Rough Boys are used to boozing on board.
The O'Brien-Flynn-Didsbury-Houston accord
would ride the ferry to New Holland pier
and back, and forth, until emptied of beer.

I place myself strategically near
- as in Staff House, early 80s - to hear

what say Larkin and his several friends.
George and Jean Hartley flank him like book-ends,

though facing opposite ends of the ship,
Jean to calm him down, George to get the pip.
Listen: "Good god, Jean, what's this? Chateau Bum?"
"Apricot wine from the wood. Makes one numb."

Big Phil switches to a 'washing sherry',
buxom Monica beside him, merry.
"Bring on the girls", he says, beaming, "we are
all the victims of printers, and Papa".

Enter painted sirens from the Ferens.
Their classic looks would have pleased Berens-
on. Pals of Ulysses, well almost.
Wearing just seaweed - naked yet modest.
Their conversatzione was great fun:
they could love you, or kill you, with a pun.
Their names? Olivia, Alessandra.
They were Italian,
they were beautiful,
and they drank tequila slammer.

Ian Parks and Shane Rhodes tread round these bawds.
They've no fucking use for hair gel or rhyme,
yet feminine fans fall upon their swords.
"So many women, so little time".

As the party warms, bar staff get the bends.
Their t-shirts pay tribute to absent friends.
"Tell me, if you had to do it all again,
would you still fall in love with yourself?"
"Tell me, who'd you go for, women or men?
What were you looking for, fame, sex, or wealth?"

Look: 'a man said to be Andrew Marvell'
has an admirer, with something to sell:
lucrative biography, and devotion.
Who sits at maestros' feet? Andrew Motion.

George Kendrick quaffs a whiskey and tonic
mixed with local anaesthetic: "Chronic
if sipped singly, but in combination
you get that Bicycle Tyre in a Tall Tree sensation".

Blood will be spilled; huge consumption of beer.
We'll re-stage the War of Tony Flynn's Ear.
This Wild Party does not believe in Time.
We have all been restored to our prime.

PART 2   CELESTIAL RECURRENCES

A small muttering Scotch-man, Dougie Dunn
("mine's a treble!") is remembering lunch,
his husbandry of the Rumoured City bunch,
and trying to forget that launch 'fun':
tears, Hitlerian rants, small-scale walkouts,
restaurant glassings, wrestling and boxing bouts.

'There are no Russians in Russia'.
This slogan from Hull Poets' own Class War
appears once more in the downstairs loo.
Motion and O'Brien feel deja vu.

Sean scrawled wit.
Andrew was appalled by it.
"See that enigmatic graffito phrase?",
he instructed his cleaner, "please erase".

(Lord Snooty versus the Mob on the bridge
is actually Oxford v. Cambridge).

Hoot. Man overboard. A drowning wretch.
"It is not the owl", it is Tony Petch.
A kind of whiskered social worker in verse.
Only case-committees could have penned his ditties;

only he could make them ten times worse.

Ah, Margot, Margot, Margot!
You should have been published by Virago.
Femme Fatale of this locale;
black nailpolish, purple eyeshadow.

Eros-wisdom priced far above rubies
is communicated by M.Juby's
spirit-guides: Eva Braun, Lou Reed, Tebbit,
the whole full moon love-lore bit.

She wears a golden razor on a chain,
and still has married men on the brain.
Tearfully swigging her 6th white wine,
she stoops to puke in handbags. "Total swine",

. she dismisses their wives, "frightful cows".
There she is, our Rebel Without a Blouse.
(A troubled relationship with mother
led to bare boobs on a chapbook cover).

There's a duel: T. Paulin against A. Thwaite,
the Oirish Ranter versus Larkin's Mate,
intent on settling the Late Show score
and resolving who is the biggest bore.

Weapons? Trifle, and remaindered copies,
thrown with insults, spit, and old Hush Puppies.
They end up covered in blancmange, a mess.
Who won? How little folk care. We care less.

But a critic cares. And so, down below,
a Dry Sailor pens another dull review.
Like that scene in the lost Ken Russell film,
                    'The Poetry Lovers',
naked wrestling with a slim white volume,
then Ian Gregson rejoins his band of brothers.

These poets in their youth would read aloud

from each others' notebooks, and scorn the crowd,
enthused by visions - success, what might be -
free at last, to be chained to poetry.

Part-librarians,
part-barbarians,
they called upon the Revising Powers
and argued the toss into the early hours,

life and art heightened, as through a prism,
during which they 'disgust' socialism.
"Delicate conversations of years gone by",
typing the life. La Vie Poesie.

All the stress, anxiety, madness, sulks,
manic arias, and burgeoning bulks,
depressions, money's Black Hole, lost promise,
lost relationships, Mr-Mrs-Miss,

all disappointments, are turned into words.
"That rough-tongued bell, Art"? Or just blood-stained turds?
As on exercise machines, such a remit
is an agonized path to benefit.

Mental detectives and/or Trainspotters.
Obsessives, dreamers, sexist rotters.
Some are famous, their bold flags unfurled;
some just flagging, ignored by the world.

Then they dispersed, scattered by the Four Winds,
becoming figures of differing kinds.
But I think of them in jackets and boaters,
all shades and sizes: slim ones and bloaters,

waltzing Paris-like boulevards, and then
in cafes fit for Unter den Linden.
"Argosies of magic sail" (Tennyson)
float by. I admit to total fiction.

This orgy concludes, the way I think best

for Hull Poets: a mud-diving contest.
PART 3   NOSTALGIE DE LA BOUE

What turns the night has taken, and what stars!
The climactic contest empties all bars.

Well, whatever it takes. The tide's gone out.
There's a water shortage, without a doubt.
This is a real poets' competition:
losers' names are mud, without remission.

By the banks of Humber they've caroused,
and by their singing, the Mud God aroused.
Foetid and noxious, his name is 'UMBER,
part-time deity and sometime plumber.

    DEUS EX MACHINA

Fish fall from his shoulders; whale-blubber whiff
mixed with oil and sewage - this is no myth.
As coarse and mucky as a Greek satyr;
the wit, the visage of Alan Plater.

"Ladies an' Gents, ah'm used t'dealin' wi' shite.
Ah support 'Ull City. Me bark's worsen me bite.
Now hear this", quaked the god, "to 'im stroke 'er
who dives the best, all t'CDs by Blur
an' Big Phil's pass for t'Lords Pavilion
an' nowt t'do wi' my mate OBLIVION.
Cannes Awards t'poets adjudged most 'ham'
(this category is sponsored by Spam).
T'worst shull give their names to a quark
an' sign big contracts wi' Littlewood Arc.
Dive at leisure, in yer own style. Left, rait.
Bloody 'ell, they can't even piss straight".

For reasons well-known to me and to you,
there sweeps over all Nostalgie de la Boue,
a sort of mud-mania amongst swine

somehow linked to the Afflatus Divine.
Eager contestants assemble at the stern,
gibbering or smarmy, waiting their turn.
Fan of Pope, friend of Thomas 'Elegy' Gray,
the Ref. Mason's here, to see unfair play.

Cadging, cursing, and pontification,
to Arts Council cash their dedication,
some recite while exiting the boat.
Some whine, sign books, plead, sing. A few don't float.

Doug Houston is first, as if from a gun.
Degree of dive difficulty, 2.1.
Through mid-air, falling, escaping ennuie,
he describes psychedelic rhapsody:

A Vision. Jet planes with lettuce leaf wings,
their smiling pilots clothed as Pearly Kings.
Oliver Reynolds leaps in the North Sea,
and starts by swimming fast, Anglo-Welshly.

Then he sinks from sight. The outlook is grim;
those cruel Reviewing Sharks must have got him.
Next, triple salkos with a double twist.
Tonys Flynn, Griffin, Petch are stonkingly pissed.

Norman Jackson dives, like a furious gull,
refuting that It's Never Dull In Hull.
The crowd look and look, declare Jacko lost;
watery slime covers any riposte.

Quick, quick as Rahtz leaving the pinko ship,
Parks, Rhodes, Tony Flynn (once again) all strip.
Naked Full Montyists, over they go,
and get stuck in the mud? Yes, yes, and no.

Maggie Hannan plunges, her legacy
odd Thesaurus words on the BBC.
Susan Wicks is back in her student days,
plummeting to escape several ex-lays.

For drunkenness, excess, riot, smoking spliff,
whoredom, wantonness, and the like, (as if)
Jonathan Raban is tossed in a blanket
over the side, just for the Hull of it.

Captain O'Brien slurps his mug of strong beer:
"I'm clearly in fucking Noddyland here".
He's a big Hull Cheese, ace submariner,
Bluto to Flynn's Popeye, a frightener.

His bold mission to circumnavigate
Pearson Park duck pond was, sad to relate,
sunk by democratic show of hands,
and the Deregulated Muse's horrible demands.

The Mutiny Poets take grog and walk the plank,
drinking Sean's health, pausing only to thank
him for not even noticing their works.
Then the bearded bard speaks: "Just jump, you birks!"

The body, the work, of Andrew Motion.
Soothing and wet, like calamine lotion.
He calls for Hoyles' Cantharadine Balm;
he calls for 3 cheers, then for dead calm.

The mud nymphs are moist, expecting Hylas.
Andrew steps from his dress, blows them a kiss.
Promising, or threatening, to come back,
he elegantly arcs. His head goes crack.

The crowd can see mild ectoplasm.
He gave the Muse an Oxbridge orgasm.
To true poets' whiskey, he was water. Eh?
He goes to Higher Realms. UEA.

While the contest concludes, hark to the Guest
of Honour: of poet-fanciers, the best.
"Happy to be here", Neil Astley the Great,
this di-versified ship's Laughtonesque First Mate.

"Hail Bloodaxe! Whose cutting edge I still defend,
with whom your careers began, and shall end.
For you all, another list of Banned Words,
and royalty cheques with which to feed birds.

You've asked me here to present the prizes.
My verdict will come with no surprises.
And who here deserves Nobel Prize-winning wealth?
Like Napoleon, I shall crown...MYSELF!"

At this point, thrice woe! He goes overboard.
Poets' spirits, and bank balances, soared.
But when shall a 'chumpion' of our own
arise, and be crowned on Terry Street stone?

As if in answer to Hullite prayers,
one man amongst these gentlefolk and players
commands the laurel wreath and traffic cone:
the chump, the worst, the most accident-prone.

 Monocentrically totemistic stuff!
The Mud God calls out - "It's ROGER McGOUGH!"
Back to Barmy Drain tepid echoes roll,
and McGough is hailed Poetic Arsehole.

The quaint old Scouser infiltrates the place,
a veil of fog and joy frames his kind face.
His histrionic gifts are undiminished,
the crowd thankful - thankful that he's finished.

A billion boaters are whirled on high.
Tremendous hurrahs rend open the sky.
As night dwindles, sparkling rockets fly,
speed through the air and beautifully die.

'Umber burps: "Eeh, ah've supped sum ale toneet".
He sinks back into his element, tight.
Nothing he said can be believed;
the real prizes go to the less deceived.
            DEUS EXEAT

                        sticking
watch and clock second hands resume ticking.

Some poets are sleeping it off.
Some are having it off.
Some are sleeping in the river bed.
Some are dreaming of our Laureate, Ted.

Carry on, Hull Poets! 'Til your number
exceeds the wading birds of the Humber,
until a campaign in the local paper
for the Bete Noire Poetry Skyscraper.

Carry on 'til this Dublin of England sneezes,
and cures all known poetic diseases.
Until the South Bank Show comes live from here,
and Melvyn's transvestized in the Polar Bear.

The party's over. It's time to get real.
The tired city rests its jewels. Yet I feel
Larkin's blessing. Or is he taking the piss?
"A triumph for you to have finished this".

linda k.
Hull, England

Homage to Saint Jude

Tracing veins in the columns, beneath the halo
slung around a wrist, the jilted hang

with heavy heads. Our jackal mouths quilted
too late. With the jinx of my luck, ravens

jabber in yews; feathers like cypress leaves,
falling dead in a surprise summer freeze.

Letters wing their way heavenwards, as if to prove
the journey can be made safely. They

flutter down defeated. Caught in boughs, a
constantly battering wind shreds each phrase.

Only single words remain, drifting
from corner, to stone, to rest

beneath the branches of a hawthorn. Roman numerals
denote the years, etched in shadow,

propped up against a red brick wall.
Clawing vine, clutching the cracks,

watched by fancy draining pipes, crawling
through the gap. Between finger and loop,

a fist of soil stains white
gasps of rice. Reverting too familiar

scars, stamped across the moon's stone face.
She shifts out from cupped hands,

tickled by naked elbows, wagging fingers.
The night time tapping of

self-conscious trees. Bowing to all those safely bedded
below the silent slab of yard.

Inland

I am looking
Out on a plane with no landmark
Except for a footstep
Immediately before me. This silence
Is what I expected; dead
With vision blind to its own prophecies.
The island is surrounded.
I am certain to step on
A causeway of history with which I am too familiar
To shed one skin without another
Selling as a replica. This monument
Poses in a coat of white lime,
The cheek to turn time to favour
The relic rather than mind
It is impossible to dig. These grooves
The worms turn to runes. I run
Each face over with a fingertip
To know heritage is a myth.

seamus curran
London, England

SEA WOMAN

Down towards the sea through forest grass and bramble
crushed violets underfoot and blackened leaves
from a long dead season he followed on
as she sure-footed stepped through unmapped ways
cleared hanging branch and briar where birds took wing
with lawless squawks and shrill exchange of whistles
and the resin-oozing barks let flood through the air clear fragrance.

Yet still in her keen nostrils the long green seamless sea
smelled salty deep from beyond the sparse-grassed banks
and sea-worn hollows where she had loosed her hair
and unstuck the clinging seaweed from her thigh
coiled up like a shelled sea fish in a mud-cracked emptied pool
and quietly conversed the evening long with the broad-backed swelling waters
till they grew dying in her ears and echoed her low breathing.

TAXI RIDE

This is what life appeared like once;
an early morning field full of light,
a dew winking in the soft stillness,
a fan of sunlight between branches.

Now the reminder along the city road --
a slanted, broken light through the park trees--
throws back a line to those more sheltered days
dense with mysterious quiet, that was not

then a mystery. Here is only a quick glimpse,
hurried through the low-roofed window
of a taxi. You are bent across the back seat,
your head askew. The streams of traffic

are an armoured population on the move.
Each bump abruptly jolts your body's
thinly-covered bones. The field once slanted up,
its line was a bright curve

over which the sky is mounted, forgetful,
as your body is now, sliding from the edge
of the seat, your stick at a haphazard angle.
Snatches of the winter blue sky escape

over roof-tops, between railings, beyond trees,
like tempting routes to freedom, a flag
limitlessly waved and hardly diminished
by office blocks or high-rise dwellings.

That sky goes back. It's not the end
of the rainbow we want, but the point
at which we started. Rolling on
in the taxi to the hospital, your head

is a gaunt statue, holding out amongst

this wayward flux. Life appeared once
like a field with the sun in it.
But there is not time now to look, or ponder.

GOOD FRIDAY

What was so good about Good Friday--
imminent thorns in the first sun,
the disconsolate half-light of the garden,
the purple passage of the priest
with his train of attendants,
the incense whisper and the bells
of benediction; after the kneeling
and standing under the order of ritual.

The first day of the Easter holidays
we had our chores laid out at home.
I grumbled under sacks of cut leaves and dust
the brush swept up. I cursed the tidy minds
of spring cleaners and the family's home-proud effort.
I made my burden longer by restless stalling.

In '91, in the hospice, your flesh
is mottled alabaster drawn on fine-wrought bones.
The high slope of the brow descends
to the deepening pools of the eyes
and the feet grow soft and bloodless
till they appear like the feet of statues.
Your sweat smells deep as nature.
It exudes the intimacy of your pain.

Now your wandering days are over.
What is so good about Good Friday?

ASHES

Your sealed casket will be air-flown.
What can I say of this?
Past promise is the passage of ashes.

I would bury them under a tree.
But the tree will be the mind
with its foliage full of tongues
tuned to the force of seasons;
the profit and the loss.

Is there only a stone
with grass growing about it--
not even the memory of a foot?
No statuary of survival?
Here there are no idols.
The tongue grows rusty
desiring a repeated communion.
It is all over

though all else remains?
For now things speak
of past destinations.
But objects have no soul
though they speak of what is,
after all, my home.

Broken things or cracked things
or stained things, with their
thunder-cloud baggage
cannot be allowed to annihilate
the life that takes shape
after a rainstorm.

Your brow is now ash.
The cerebral storm is over.

FALSE SPRING

Must not starve or recoil
from the morning, faintly
coming under the blind.
Traces of whiskey stir
the blanketed loins
and there is nothing
to breakfast on.
Must not starve the day out
like yesterday. Must make
it to the supermarket.
Must buy something green
with vitamins intact
to avoid cold sores, colds
and feeling lax.
Though whiskey gives the energy back
must not buy that.
Must check out the bank.
Must count the pennies
and not go mad.

Saturday, dull as dishwater
so far, a gloom on the streets
like a nicotine filter
and rain thin as a distant whisper,
through which a million
wet pinheads trickle and drop.

Day to night clings
like the cold sweat on the sheets.
Sunlight is penetrated by February winds.
You cling to sleep
like to a dead lover.
Time steps up
to be accounted for.
When will the glands flood
the wintry anatomy?

When will the sap rise?
When will the new year mate
with the old, step away
from the long shadow, step out
from under the stone?
What would you expect from nature --
some breathtaking metaphor?

TO LISA

O dear. O dear
the drink has made me criminally hopeful.
You plan a thousand plans
over pints of stout in a London pub
on St.Patrick's day. And there are doleful
melancholic things we say between the lines.
We are getting on a bit now. Let us not lie.
But hopeful, hopeful are the plans you inscribe.

Everything is coming apart.
There are no good vibes to fix a late truce
between me and a lover. And your husband
is amidst a family squabble and his mother
on the point of death and there are other
problems on the theme of work. Is there any use
in making pints of Murphys' speak the truth?
The truth is a man with a wilting shamrock
drinking himself into a furore of handshakes.

Years come and go and go it seems
and more is packed into them, 'till it is a case-
history staring back; always a case of being
more or less the same in a world changing.
Would we have given much for it to stay the same
as we walk through London streets like memory lanes
on a Sunday, when it's empty enough to think.
Still plan on plan makes positive future dates.

All in all life's planning seems better
than following lifes accidents to the letter,
even if the plans un-stitch themselves according to the
                                future.
Some day, perhaps we'll look back, aware
that all our talk was a way of making do.
More than less was enough 'till we'd forget
that time had caught us in its factual net.

But without being too bent on the philosophic,
after a few pints and cunning swerves from the melancholic
we are as we always were, the same; out-stepping
time's footsteps that would tell us we are someone other.

STONES

Stones upon stones. A history shared with stones.
The ancients buried in the burial mound,
where the sun's solstice passes
over the doorway, sleeks down the passageway
and rubs the centre of the floor to one candlepower.
So do the chosen still come at the appointed hour
to stand full circle in the bell-like enclosure,
to open the eye, like that of an ancestor,
in a territory, legendary, historical,
with its crosses and towers, its battle on the river.
Stones so stubborn were still bent to the will
of the builders of houses, walls and graves.

LANGUAGE LESSONS

You cover your tracks well.
You don't say no to a man when you mean yes.
You flirt when life comes on like a flirtatious knack.
But what sort of man would end up in your lap?
Some young man with his laces undone,
whose by-word spells a stalling, hidden sex?

Who are you in your heavy eye makeup?
You could play mother with your nurse's bluntness.
There's stories at your fingertips, with beer in hand.
A German 'student doctor picks up on your slang.
But he says' knickered' for 'knackered'.
You tell him a French friend once rang you up
and she said she was 'naked'.
But that's how English gets from Finglas
to the German operating-table.

peter didsbury
Hull, Enland

CEMETERY CLEARANCE

Some kind of scheme, I suppose.
Our Lady of the Bolt-Croppers,
tall and how beautifully trousered,
stands smiling among the stones.
Behind her, in the sere grasses of autumn,
in the low drifting smoke of small fires,
her young men crawl
at her bidding among the dead.
Spirits and wonders!
To whatever is able to will to invest
with such an image of the fitness of things
even this sorry enterprise
honour and praise is for ever abundantly due.

joanne pearson
York, England

"Message to a Friend"*

He knows
I am a troubled soul tonight.
My mind and body jangle.
In a constant state of flux,
unable to relax.

Friendship misunderstandings
left a sour taste
in my throat.
Disturbed and disconcerted.
Ripped a dress apart,
torn and ruined.

Pat Metheny and Charlie Haden
in the background
do not
still anxiety.

The pretty throws
across the bed
are funeral flowers
of ruby red
from dark blood
dripping from my legs.

Attempts to disembowel
this bitter ache
with an elegy.

*From Beyond the Missouri Sky

charles bukowski
(1920-1994) Los Angeles, USA

cheer up

I never went to see him, maybe I should have. but I asked him once and he said, "no, you're not crazy, you're one of the sanest men I've ever met," which, of course, is not very flattering.

he's not only a shrink but he runs a nightclub and he also asks me if there is anything I might need in the way of drugs or women and my answer is 'no' to both -- they seem to arrive anyhow.

"yeah," he says, "it's like I told you: you don't need me."

we are at the racetrack bar -- between races, of course.

"I really got a strange one now," he tells me, "a hockey goalie. he tells me he has these dreams. only in the dreams these hockey pucks come flying toward him as they do they change into flying pussies with horrible orifices which screech at him. whatcha think of that one?"

"sounds like a gentleman who wants to be a homosexual but doesn't know how. by the way, isn't it improper to discuss a patient's case at a racetrack bar?"

"it's people worrying about doing the 'improper' that most often brings them to the psychiatrist's couch."

"listen," I say, "what's proper here is that I need a winner. the one horse is best on paper but it's 7 furlongs and he's going to have to rush up to keep getting shit off from the inside, meanwhile the outside horse is going to break free and easy and he'll pick it up when he wants to. I'm going for the outside horse."

"I think you're wrong. the inside horse has won 8 out of ten against class. your horse won only its maiden race."

I tell him it's been nice for the free consultation and go bet forty win on the outside at 2 to one. the inside is even money.
I walk over to the monitor and watch the race.

pain like an old black and white snapshot

the dead dogs of Normandy -- twilight in Missouri -
the dead dogs of nowhere -- empty gas pump -
the dead dogs of the walls and the purple sun -
lights
the dead dogs of Nirvana -- Felschamp with broken
ankle -
the dead dogs of our love the dead vanilla dogs
with icecream eyes -- the shy plant in the north
yard -

dogs

the aviator dogs the president dogs the dogs that
crawl the wallpaper -- an early glimpse of November -
the dogs that burn the town down the dogs who kick
forty yard field goals -- promise sings like a
snake -

I was a young dog of 23 and you a beautiful woman
of 35
cunting me burning me and leaving me alone at 11 p.m.
12 a.m. 3 a.m. 7 a.m. 2 days 3 days 4 days
my guts bleeding across the avenues -- the swan
circles and waits -

now I'm and old man and you've been dead 26 years

and often I'm alone at noon at 5 p.m. 5 a.m. 6:30
p.m. 2 a.m.

I walk across unsolved territories
often getting lost and trapped and fooled again
but you were the first
dog
to take that special bite in that first way

now
further courtesanships have helped bury the
yell

now
sometimes
it can even be summer in Cleveland,
Ohio.

that's where they came from

dead flowers in a bowl looking across at me in a room
too dark because I do not light, they have shut off
the water again and are banging on the pipes, this is
a crazy house, they raided last night and I would not
let them in, the chain held and I moved the sofa against
the door and called my lawyer and the fat whore cried
and at last they went away; this Sunday drags its snake-
body in and out of sockets, the phone rings leaping
across the couch like a dog, and right away I think
I have been poisoned and I walk over to the flowers
and my hands are too weak to pull them out, not now
so white white so pink pink but rotten dead dead
and the squawk of a jay rips through the leaves like
cannonfire from a Napoleonic age, and I stand
dead flowers and sunlight burning my whiteness
a thousand tombstones out of glory and I take the
flowers white not so white pink not so pink
like turning out a light and I throw them throw them
throw them out. OUT and I move and answer the
phone and a voice says HAPPY BIRTHDAY DARLING.

regrets of a sort..

I've written all these
just using the language
I know
even when it became
laboriously near to
listening to your
neighbour
over the
backyard fence.

I like the language:
the curl of the
word
the sensation
of a
tasty
almost never-used
beauty
a near-virgin
word.

there are many
of them.

at times
I read the dictionary
marvelling
at the totality of
the untouched
backlog.

there's a force
there
properly used
would make
all I've said
almost
useless

yet
when I consider
the others
who have delved into this
backlog

the educated
the schooled
the
knowing?

it
doesn't appear to
work

or have they
chosen
the wrong
words?
for fashion?
for dictate?

and without the
luck of taste
and
style?

Whatever,
the users
have discouraged me
with
vocabulary
as if it were
a shield
for pretenders

and so
for the moment
I am caught
with this
left with
this

and since you
have come
this
far

so
are you.

let's hope
we can all
recover from
this.

darlings of the word

2 poets from San Francisco (one
quite famous) are down here
and she's gone out to hear
them.

I'm glad
at the moment
that
I don't have to
read
anymore.

I never typed this
stuff
to get up and
read it to
the mob.

I used to read for the
$$$
it got the rent and the
drink
but when I hear of the
famous and the well-fed
still doing it
I marvel with
askance
at thair act.

it has always seemed
curious to me
that
the poets were
(are) such
extroverts

they love to
get up and
warble.

I once asked a
poet about this
<u>itch</u>
and he told me:

"it's an old art-
form. poets throughout
the centuries past

used to walk up and
down the streets
singing their works,
their madrigals. poetry
belongs to the people."

"I don't know about that,"
I said, "but I guess even
writing for the printed
page is a form of
vanity."

"poetry belongs to the
people," he
repeated.

"all right," I said,
"forget it..."

if I had wanted to be
an actor
I would have gone
to Hollywood.

the first act is
in the typing

and all that follows
is
propaganda:

the
teachings
the

teachers
the readings never

will match what
began it...

2 poets from San
Francisco are
down here
now

so
far
down
here

now.

norman jackson
Hull, England

Feeding the Birds

Mr Crow! Mr Crow!
My coarse cry brings them down
To the garden wall.
After the offal, the chicken parts,
Food the cat won't eat
Is chucked over.
Our neighbours think I'm a bird.
Chesty with tobacco and a Bovril breakfast,
I stand near the pond, croaking in
These blocks of beak and claw.
They don't fly, they drop from the trees
Like black clouds of rain.
Carrion, omens of something gone wrong.

andy fletcher
Hull, England

Fifteen

In the cloakroom at school
I kissed a boy full on the lips.

I was fifteen at the time
and we'd have done it again
if we hadn't been caught.

I used to imagine him
swollen with boredom, his
nakedness a parachute on which
he descended from a deep blue sky.

Afterwards, I had to wear
a jacket of shame, listen
to calls of 'homo' and 'queer'.

I couldn't separate truth from truth.

I crept away into an innocent
forest where coats hung from
the branches.

The big-muscled boy
with soft skin would appear
round a tree trunk -

And we'd reach for each other
and kiss and kiss and kiss.

geoff stevens
West Bromwich, England

Personally Defaced by Joe Orton

After the moustache
and the spectacles
with their heavy frames
your insertions escalated
began to draw in
the borrowers' breath
redden a few faces.
Putting monkey faces
between the petals
in Collins Guide to Rises
was a schoolboy prank
but changing Emlyn Williams'
play to "Fucked by Monty"
was very naughty for 1962
not to mention that
your books were overdue.
So you were sent inside.
Hope it taught you
to respect the Library!

gerald locklin
Long Beach, USA

bud powell on verve
(for bob austin)

i always had trouble with the fast guys--
charlie parker, coleman hawkins, bud powell--
i guess i was a young romantic in search of
the lyrical, rhapsodic and climactic--stan
kenton, gerald wilson, coltrane, ahmad jamal--
the brooding miles who *really* slowed things
down and took them overseas. but now the
liner notes instruct my ear in the "romantic
agony" of improvisation at a breakneck pace:
the challenge of it, living on the brink of
failure, the incomparable concentration on
coordination of brain, heart, and fingers,
context of the rhythm section, historical
gestalt, the journey taking him from classically
trained child of a musician through the smoke
and drugs of urban blues clubs to the left-bank
caves where his piano would personify *le jazz hot*.
as with hart crane, it was artistry within a
crumbling tower, the crystal peal of aching bells.
i haven't spent my obligatory april in paris yet, but
i have known the bareness of december in the
gardens there. as caillebotte perceived, it
sometimes rains on Sundays on parisian boulevards.
time has a way of getting out of 4/4 joint, and
sometimes it is best that we just take it somewhere; sometimes it's the last control we ever
exercise. sometimes the stars are *only* in our
eyes, and sometimes we no longer have the lungs
to contemplate ascending the steep stairway to the
end of night. eventually even bud powell has to
slow things down and meditate, grown elegiac:
c'est la vie; it was just one of those things;
it never even entered my mind.

it never entered his mind.
it never entered ours.

and then it does.

and sometimes not so tenderly.

this guy and i are

talking behind closed doors
about how much more frequently
plain women could get laid
if only they could be counted on
not to take it seriously
and not to tell anyone,

but later it occurs to me
i might have had
a lot more sex myself
over the years
if i hadn't felt the need
to commit every such occasion
to print.

easier than swimming laps

in the next life,
no matter whether i end up
in the northern or southern hemisphere,
i think (it being eternity and all that,
and thus not involving much threat of
dying prematurely) that i just may
go back to drinking and stay half-
shitfaced all the goddamn time.

depressing books

reading depressing books
never used to depress me.
then one day i noticed that
depressing books had begun
to depress me. now i am
at this stage at which reading
depressing books still
depresses me.

i have no idea whether
or for how long
reading depressing books will
continue to depress me.

the pendulum swings off its hinge

i'm reading hundreds of essays
by teenagers who almost unanimously agree
that their parents are abridging
their god-given right
to make all decisions,
major or minor,
for themselves,

and it occurs to me
that i can't remember at their age
ever being informed that i had
any rights at all.

he leads by example
(for g.h.)

my friend has been fighting cancer.
he tells me he just finished
heavy-duty radiation treatments,
and the side effects weren't pleasant,
but he saw a lot of people
in the waiting room who were
worse off than he was.
"i was able," he tells me,
" to ride my bike to and from
the sessions."

now I know this guy doesn't ride
his bike the way I would,
like a grandfather tooling around
the neighbourhood streets,
waving to toddlers,
but like a triathlon competitor,
pumping away for all he's worth
up miles of asphalt. so I say,

"jesus, pal, i've never heard of
anyone who rode his bike to radiation
therapy---you must be doing great".

"nah," he says," I can tell i'm weaker:
i'm using lighter weights and doing
fewer reps in the gym."

his attitude is, this thing can kill me
but it can't change the way I choose to live,

which proves there's such a thing
as catholic existentialism
because his religion, quietly practiced,
is another thing sustaining him.

he's a great guy with everything to live for:
his talent, his kids, an exceptionally good
marriage. he's had to struggle all his life,
but that's another thing that's strengthened him.
ultimately, though, who can account for spirit,
why some have it, seemingly so few,
and why the others don't.

i'd been laying off my own workouts,
telling myself i needed to rest
a few minor aches and pains,
but after we got off the phone,
i headed for the y.m.c.a.

john james audubon: <u>whooping crane</u>

look at me lift one foot.
i like to do that.
i like how long
every bit of us is.

i think i'll take
this lizard in my beak.
the brightly striped one.
i think i'll eat this one.
i left the plainer one for dead,
belly up,
and soft beneath the chin.

afterwards i'll have a sip
or two of the pond.
maybe a dip.
and aren't those leaves lovely?
i'm having a very nice day,
thank you,
another one.

vishnu, siem reap , 9th century

a man needs many arms.
a god needs even more,
or none at all.

not from dust came we,
but water. we crawled
up on the land. we ruled
it without our knowledge. then
we thought to think about ourselves.

we had strong legs
to stand on, so we would

not fall off of the spinning
earth. our heads were pillars
also, to support the atmosphere
and sky. we mastered sleight - of -
hand. we began to believe our
own magic.

we had a tendency to go too far.

The Riots

I see Cowboy Bob come through the threshold of the Vegas Room and, thinking it may be instructive to the young people in the booth, I wave to him to please join us. Before he has a chance to object, I signal the bartender to give him a beer on me. Bob is a proud man---rather than be in anyone's debt he would buy the bar a round with his food money. I know for a fact he has partaken of his dog's food rather than request an (easily granted) loan from any of us. During an unusually traumatic and masculinity-threatening divorce he endured, I had to write a judge to secure his release from a mental ward. I introduce him now to our booth, as I did then to the magistrate, as " the last sane man in Long Beach".

"So, Bob, " I say,"where were you during the riots? " I expect to hear that he was two hundred miles from L.A. at Murrieta Hot Springs, where he has been doing a lot of carpentry for a contractor the last few years, but instead he says,

"Hey, I was up in Beverley Hills visiting with my ex-wife-the-banker when the verdict was announced.I didn't necessarily expect any major trouble,but I discerned the freeways weren't even moving. So I started down La Cienega, still not anticipating any hassles, but not exactly naked and defenceless. I had Maggot, my pup,riding shotgun with me,of course,and I was also packing..." He proceeds to inventory an arsenal.

"If it had been you that the mob had tried to pull from the truck, "I say, "instead of that poor Reginald Denny, the riots might have been over before they ever got started."

"Well, I did have my twelve-gauge featured rather prominently up front, but it still took three hours to get home. The real fun started the next night, though, when I spent the rest of the weekend camped out with the Marines."

"You mean this time they actually let you re-up like you tried to do for Desert Storm?"

"Nah... but you know what this piece of cardboard with the stick-um on the back is?... It's a Press Card from *The Orange County Register* that a buddy of mine who was covering the rodeo procured for me. On a hunch, I hadn't thrown it out. So when I heard the guys from Pendleton hed taken up positions downtown I hopped in my truck and hightailed it down Seventh Street. Naturally I was immediately headed off by three police cars. The first thing they asked me was, ' Hey are you crazy?' "

" 'Hell no, ' I said,' I'm on assignment.' And I pointed to the Press Card I had stuck to my forehead. So the cop said, 'Well, you were driving like a bat out of hell, 'and I said, ' That's 'cause I'm scared shitless. You don't think I asked for this assignment, do you? That would be really mean I must be nuts.'

" At least lay that shotgun on the floor. You know damn well you people aren't supposed to be armed."

"Do you blame me?"

"Did I *say* I blamed you? Just keep any firepower well out of sight. And if you're determined to run anybody over between here and Atlantic, make sure they're not on *our* side..."

"So did you observe any incidents?"

"There wasn't much fucking with the Marines. I did overhear one exchange I'll never forget. There was a certain amount of jiving going on between young black civilians and young black marines. And, of course, the young black marines, when they couldn't avoid the dialogue altogether, would try to say just enough in street-talk to indicate that sure, they recognized their solidarity with their brothers, but that their brothers would have to understand that they were not about to leave themselves vulnerable to courts martial. But there was one older black guy standing guard there with his automatic rifle, not saying anything, just kind of keeping the entire scene under surveillance. So here comes one of those street dudes starting to sidle up to him to launch into the sweet-talk, and the old marine adjusts his weapon almost imperceptibly and says, ' You come one step closer or make one more noise and I'm gonna blow your fuckin' head off.'"

" That kind of put a damper on the conversation?"

" That kind of brought an instant silence to the area."

"I guess *this* place closed down during the curfew?"

"All the joints did, except, ironically, the lesbian bar down the street. I spent the last night of the cufew in there because everything had gone pretty dull outside. It was the first time they'd ever acted glad to see me. I bought a drink when I arrived and it was the last one I paid for all night. I guess the cops had come by earlier in the evening and told the owners they'd leave it up to them if they felt safe staying open. It's practically a private club anyway."

"No double standard there."

Cowboy Bob shrugs, "Speaking of which, your university go belly-up yet? I don't mean the curfew; I mean Chapter Eleven."

" Pretty damn close."

"Why don't you get rid of the frills?"

"They're long gone, Bob. They're down to two daytime maintenance men, for instance."

"I'm not talking about maintenance. Don't you still have a Women's Studies department and a black, oh, excuse me, African American Studies department and all the other special interest advocacy departments?"

"Hell, Bob, you know they'll be the last to go."

"Well, there you have it. The riots didn't get near your neighbourhood, did they?"

"It's such a small town that you're never very far from where someone is shooting someone else, even on a regular weekend. But, no, we certainly weren't in the center of things. On the other hand, even in our neighbourhood banks and gas stations and liquor stores were acting nervous and closing early. I made sure I had a full tank and a healthy liquor cabinet. I don't have a gun but I doubt I'd have to walk far to borrow one."

"My wife and I did have to drive into Signal Hill on Friday afternoon to pick up my little boy from where the school busses were dropping him and the other fifth graders off after the week of camping in the mountains. That DMV office was still smoldering a couple of blocks away. There was a strong police presence at the school, but naturally my wife got stubborn about what street to turn up and I let her have her way even though I knew she was wrong. So we ended up on this side of the street with no other traffic and five young guys loitering on the next street corner. I figured we could expect either five bricks through the side window or five beer bottles or that they would try to block the car and drag us out of it. So I hit the accelerator: if anyone wanted to step in front of my hurtling vehicle, he'd have to do it knowing there's no way I can play Mr Nice Guy and apply the brakes before putting him into orbit. But no flying objects, nothing. Maybe the cops had just been past; maybe they were just okay guys. It was not a good time to overestimate the milk of human kindness."

"Well, look", Bob says, "I appreciate the beers and you better let me return the favor soon, because I don't like being in any man's debt for long. I'm hoping in fact, to be able to write a letter that will get you out of the nut house one of these days."

"My feminist colleagues are doing their best to afford you that oppertunity."

"Now, as much as I enjoy solving the world's problems, it is unfortunately necessary that I see that guy who just came through the door about the possibility of some cabinet-making for the new house he's builing."

"Good luck, Bob, " I say; "it's always a pleasure jawing with you."

* * *

"*That,*" says one of the young people, "*was the same sane man in Long Beach?*"

"We could probably, "I say "extend the boundaries."

"He's a racist, "someone says.

"No, "I say, "he sets high standards of self-reliance for all men. Like Ralph Waldo Emerson. He's one of the least racist people I know."

"What's the sanity bullshit?"

"I mean his rationality is in balance with his sociobiological imperatives."

It's a good time to go get another vodka tonic.

labi siffre
Abergavenny, Wales

Workshop

Let's not write about Omagh, Co Tyrone
August 14th in the year of our Lord 1998
and the pregnant woman whose legs were blown off
and the 29 dead and the hundreds wounded
and the severed limbs we didn't see on TV

Let's not reach for adjectives to express the concern
we all feel   nor comfort ourselves   please
with poems about our longing
for peace and brotherhood
and sisterhood too
'cause that's not what poets are supposed to do

Hold on to your craft in metaphor
a parallel score obscure enough
to be universally true   about clouds
and rivers   and God perhaps

That nice chap Tony Blair could barely express his feelings
and the queen, God bless her, was horrified
at these "appalling murders" as we all were
waiting for the sports results
and the movie

South Africa 24
New Zealand 23

Besides   anything else   would be merely
politically correct

Inadequate Pronouns

At odds with restraint every night he beat him senseless
with love   sledge-hammer kisses   caresses ploughing
furrows of blood   pelvic thrusts that burst the mattress
threatened the bed's legs   the ochre stained floor
the apartment below   quivering

raw his nipples blazed scarlet pyramids to his breath
his tongue his teeth caressed his flesh like pumice
his hands moulded pulled squeezed threatened
promised bruised inserted insisted   till vowels

burst from his lips in an agony of pleasure and
helpless he came   then   helpless
He came

Don't Worry Baby

Naked black and permanently erect
the cannon 'though ceremonial are vigilant
staring out to sea
their main concern is Afrika
getting closer

We crunch our way through the litter of skull fragments
carpeting the street   blood and brains
stick to our feet   but none of their memories suggest
a worthwhile course of action we have courage to pursue

Below   the beach is flooded with summer
sun-beds umbrellas families   like the two fat guys
up to their waists in Mediterranean   exchanging bodily fluids
I'd like to be between them   yes

But don't worry
with AIDS and armaments more readily available
than bread   you have little to fear
from the dark continent

Affirmation
(for Pride '99)

Take heart
Our love is stronger
than their fear

The logic of my hand in yours
a shield
against their willful ignorance

Tomorrow they will hate us
naturally   for the comfort
of arrogance is all they possess

Ten thousand billion voices raised
to claim our love is wrong
pretended   sick   impure

Tomorrow I will love you
as I love you now
and more

carol coiffait
Welton, England

I Guess It's Been a Long Time Since I Held My Mother's Hand

That first Christmas
after Father died
you
had to write the cards
and tried
with your short name
writ large
to fill each
space.

I watched you
shrink
into yourself;
to husband
what was left
for you
in life.
Yet another small
and un-manned
wife.

And once
in those first weeks
you let me
take your hand.
I tell you
I was shaken
by its breadth
its strength.

Yes, once
four years ago
I held
your hand.

Brave

I know how to kill a dog, stop a lion
in its tracks, suck the venom from a bite.

I know how to swim on my back, cradle
your head on my left shoulder, buoy up
your body with my hip, gain momentum
with one arm and powerful kicks.

And I know how to douse a blazing pan
of chips, with lid or dampened cloth, pull you
to the floor to suck in air beneath the smoke.

I know how to fling you to the ground with
me on top, to protect you from the blast
the flying glass, the rocks.

I know how to stick the boot in, use teeth
and fists, when muggers spring.

I know enough to tote a knife, a crowbar
and a rope, to cut you free, to prise, then
drag you from a crumpled car.

I know also how to live a lie, put
a good face on things, appear to thrive, then
before your very eyes, inch by painful
inch, to slowly die.

Hide And Seek

Wind riffles through the house,
it is searching for evidence of you.

Already it has taken fingerprints
from all the books you read

And from the beds and carpets,
three grammes of dust, for analysis.

Under the roof, it detects music;
the high notes are shaken, tested

But the bass notes are folded
left in a corner, pending enquiries.

Try as it might, it cannot trace your smell
but it has found the space you occupied

Beneath my ribs; completely missed
the private cinema
behind my eyes.

His Voice And Flesh Are Gone or It's A Long Way To Wakefield

If the square root of Heaven
is really seven, (your birthday)
Why couldn't you stay seven times seven
Long enough to take your daughter
(two times nine) for her birthday meal
and a glass of wine?

If Heaven is blue and Hell is yellow
The quilt is green for my fine fellow.

If pye-r-squared is a monocycle wheel
Better buy a bicycle, get a better deal
Better buy a tandem or a trike.,
A scooter or a Saab
And drive all night

Six foot by three, six foot by three
Martha and Mary sitting up a tree
Six foot by three, six foot by three
Swinging their legs to the enth degree.

Over the hills and a great way off
At the rainbow's end it's sniff sniff, cough.
Call him quickly
Call him slow
Call him softly
He won't go...

Martha and Mary sitting up a tree
By an unmarked grave, six foot by three
Alone in Wakefield Cemetery.

Photographic Evidence

The face I search for changes
but it's always you
or your brother.
This old plastic bag
with the legend SPAR on it,
spills a restless family
of small boys across my carpet
random as windfalls
some plump and rosy
some thin, a little worse for wear
but all smiling:

Except for you at four
alone in a field
Except for you at nine
kneeling by the dog
Except for you at twenty-one
avoiding the camera's eye.
You are about to leave the nest
and twitching to be gone
with your inheritance
of restlessness.

I should have trimmed one wing,
kept you close and fed you
from sepia, to black and white
to full colour, until
you were strong enough
to blow the sun's saxophone
well beyond the millennium.

reviews

TWO NOVELLAS:
Donna Hilbert........................ 'WAITING FOR MY BABY'

Gerald Locklin........'THE FIRST TIME HE SAW PARIS'

(Event Horizon Press, 1998) pp. 324 $29.95 (unsigned), $39.95 (signed edition). Available from Event Horizon Press, PO Box 867, Desert Hot Springs, California 92240 USA.

Originally from Long Beach, Event Horizon has from 1990 onwards been a poetry press with a list containing the best of Southern California; as well as the two above authors, also Fred Voss (they first published that instant classic Goodstone), Joan Jobe Smith, and Jennifer Olds. As far as I am aware Two Novellas is their first production of complementary prose works in one volume; made relatively expensive by two colour plates and being assembled and perfect bound by hand. Whether editor/proprietor Joseph Cowles has the ambition to evolve from a small press to international publisher à la Black Sparrow Press remains to be seen, but Event Horizon is a fine showcase for a generation of native talent that has become prominent, with many readers in the U.K.

This is particularly true of Gerald Locklin, though he migrated to the West Coast in the mid-1960s from Rochester, New York via a few years as a graduate student in Tuscon, Arizona. Such factors give his work a satirical edge and 'literary' facetiousness, his narrators a humorously cynical view of their milieu (whether Los Angeles and its environs, Paris, or England) that is very entertaining while allowing far more depth of social commentary than an offhand manner might suggest. The other Lockin essential is consistent productivity over the past three decades; though most of his 78 listed titles have been chapbooks, he is one of the most widely-published figures in the States, with a mass-market paperback following in Germany. If such a career profile reminds us to some extent of the 1970s Charles Bukowski, it's worth observing that Locklin's has occured within his occuaption as university teacher, and their friendship was a mutually respectful one. Indeed, 'influence'was by no means all one-way: Buk's final novel, Pulp (1994) is clearly influenced by Locklin's much funnier and more exactly-written spoofing of Detective genre fiction, The Case of the Missing Blue Volkswagon (1984). The unpublished correspondence between the two men, held at Cal. State Long Beach library, has several enthusing references by Bukowski to "Blue Volks". I was reminded of this when reading in The First Time He Saw Paris a joking phrase recycled from the earlier novella; Long Beach is "the Paris of the New World". The casual irony of such a phrase, feeding off the glamour of the 1920s Moderns versus contemporary California, Capital City pretension versus Blue Collar writing and working, is typical Locklin.

'Jimmy Abbey', protagonist in many Locklin stories, is An American in Paris (Gershwin being one of the few Moderns not invoked by the incurably literary if irreverent narrative) during the Christmas vacation. Packing The Sun Also Rises and A Moveable Feast as well as more regular Parisian baedekers, he ironically forsakes reading for action, cramming as many Hemingwayan appetites for food, drink and sex, and depressions ("the Blackass") as time and the body allows. Descriptions of meals, snacks, drinking bouts are many; sometimes joyous, often unwise; "le roi du biere" at the Ladybird Club suffers extreme gastric remorse. The various women he encounters lead only to a rather awkward encounter with a black prostitute; as ever in fiction and in movies, no condom is used, but relax - this is the early 1970s ("Nixon is still lying"). Tourist culture, and the culture of this particular tourist, leads to some enjoyably debunking dialogue:

"Claire fixes them Scotch and Perrier.
'This is delicious', he says, 'especially after a day of le nouveau Beaujloais'...
'You must go to the Rosebud. Perhaps you will see Jean-Paul Sartre'.
'How will I know him?'
'His eyes cross badly. They say he reads two books at once.'
'I will go there'.

Experienced Locklin readers will know that he specialises in this kind of allusive and wise-cracking dialogue, particularly in exchanges between male and female characters, so that the satirical focus is sometimes on the speaker and sometimes elsewhere. He has trademarked an episodic, casual-seeming style chopped into short scenes; with these simple but flexible fictional traits, he captures The War Between Men and Women, social and political trends, dark nights of the soul and the state of the bowels. In all this, The First Time He Saw Paris is characteristic of his work. Less usual is the counterpointing of Jimmy Abbery's material concerns, where his next food and drink are coming from, with a spiritual side that surfaces whenever he is reminded of the season, Christmas, and his lapsed Catholicism (as when a quartet of Oxford gals turn down his offer of a night on the town in favour of Midnight Mass). There are clues that his binges don't satisfy a deeper hunger. But such interludes are usually presented in comic terms. Charles Bukowski once wrote of Locklin that at his best, he was a fucking delightful writer. With this novella, you can find out exactly what Bukowski meant.

Whereas Locklin's hero is a very 'driven', outside observer with an implicit dark side, 'Sandy Henderson' in Waiting for My Baby is a centered female presence surrounded by a network of supportive female friends. A much more orthodox prose technique is employed in this first-person story of a woman preparing for childbirth; preparing also for the 1960s, in low-rent Seattle, as events (the Vietnam War, the Watts Riots) and personalities (Johnson, Dr. King, Dean Martin, Mike Wallace) unfold on television or arise in conversation. These two novellas might be prime examples of gender differences in fiction. It's very unlikely that a male author could capture the lived detail of babies, networking between women, observations of mothers and daughters, attitudes, female consciousness in general, as well as Donna Hilbert does. The novella's strength is in its range of characters, from the landlady 'Mrs. Worthy' and her monstrously fat daughter 'Lurene' (hoping for a baby but settling for pierced ears), to Sheila the exotic dancer at the Cottontail Club (relax again - this is the 1960s), to the cute and smelly baby 'Messy'. Underscoring the plot is an almost Dickensian attempt to wring pathos out of the serious illness of one of the women, a 'Welfare Mother' in today's terminology, and the deaths of an orphaned kitten plus 'Namu" the whale. Tha male characters tend to be stereotyped as feckless, sexually threatening, or ridiculous, except for a fatherly postman. (Okay, the teenage 'Mirlou' in Locklin's story is also a stereotype).

More subtle than her overt plotline, which moves towards that rare thing in contemporary fiction, the happy ending, is the way in which Hilbert infuses it with larger social observations: the growing ubiquity of television, the emancipation of women from restrictive roles and assumptions, and changing sexual mores - or at least the beginnings of these current norms during the 1960s (why set a book in the recent past if not to shed light on today?). Donna Hilbert, a respected figure in Long beach writing, especially for her previous publications with Event Horizon, <u>Mansions</u> (1990) and <u>Deep Red</u> (1993), deserves a wider audience. In bookish terms, the pairing with Locklin works well, albeit on a 'Compare and Contrast' basis. Taken together, as they must be, these <u>Two Novellas</u> confirm the suspicion that men and women are two different species...and that children are a third.

Jules Smith

DENISE LEVERTOV ' SANDS OF THE WELL' (Bloodaxe)

These poems were written when Denise Levertov was in her seventies and the collection was completed the year before she died. If this suggests a recipe for cozy retrospection, think again. When she does look back, it is to challenge and analyse the memory with formidable vigour.

Her poetry is steeped in politics. She was active in the American Civil Rights Movement and she campaigned against the Vietnam War. Her poetry is spiritual. Her father was a Russian Jew who became an Anglican priest. Her poetry frequently refers to nature and the universal truths which may be found through the natural world. These influences pervade Denise Levertov's poetry but she cannot be classified as a "political" or a "spiritual" or a "nature" poet. She is all this and more. Her poetry reflects beliefs which come from a whole lifetime's experiences and influences. The themes may be complex, but she uses language with a clarity and directness which seems to elude many contemporary poets. She communicates with a voice of quiet conviction which has a powerful cumulative impact. Her intellectual energy is startling. Her most memorable poems are those which search, challenge and analyse. In 'Looking, Walking, Being' she says "Looking's a way of being."

Her beliefs are reasoned, but her response to the world is not purely cerebral. In 'The Cult of Relics' she is prepared to reconsider the blurred edges between religion and superstition and finds sympathy for those who believe. In 'The Mystery of Deep Candor' she finds magic through simplicity. It is her conviction that magic is there to be found.

In 'A South Wind' she exhorts us all to really look at our surroundings:

"Nothing much, or everything; all depends
  On how you regard it.
          On if you regard it."

This seems good advice to follow whether you are a poet or not.

Fiona Arnott

IAN PARKS 'A CLIMB THROUGH ALTERED LANDSCAPES'
(Black Sparrow Press)

The poems in this collection are well written, beautifully wrought and easily read. Each one appears as a drama in miniature. The best ones give the reader just enough to enable the imagination to run beyond the words on the page. I particularly liked 'The Disinterment' which evokes for me the romance of legends about long dead but perfectly preserved Jacobite Lords. This may or may not be the scenario, but does it matter? Its ghoulish romance is wonderfully Gothic.I also like 'The Pearl' which is almost a soliloquy and conjours up images of opulent, misshapen baroque pearls and the courtiers who wore them with panache. These are poems reminiscent of Browning in the tradition of 'My Last Duchess.' They inspire the imagination. If other poems in the collection bring less pause for thought, they are always lucid, elegant and readable.

I am puzzled by two things. At 50 pages, the collection is slim and some of the poems date back to the mid-eighties. I suppose my question is-are there any more poems, and if not, why not? I am also puzzled by the fact that despite being the protagonist of many of these dramas with passionate themes, the poet's voice is controlled, distanced and cool. This is not necessarily a fault, of course, and it contributes to the urbanity of the writing. I do not feel we hear the poet's own voice through these poems. We don't learn his thoughts, values or passions. Perhaps it was not the poet's intention that we should.

Fiona Arnott

Stephen Dobyns.......COMMON CARNAGE (Bloodaxe,1997) pp.127 £8.95
C.K Williams...............................THE VIGIL (Bloodaxe,1997) pp.78 £ 7.95
John Hartley Williams..................CANADA (Bloodaxe, 1997) pp. 127 £7.95

Shortly after C.K williams had begun a recent reading, at Hull Central Library (3 June 1998), an elderly man left his front-row seat and walked forward, saying he was sorry, he was 92 and the batteries in his hearing-aid had just failed, and then he shuffled out. It was the kind of bizarre yet all-too-human incident that might feature in a C.K Williams poem, a reminder of mortality and idiosyncrasy. The poet himself was flustered for awhile, shortly thereafter knocking over a water jug, but overall he was far more authoritative than on his previous visit to Hull, when he read with Miroslav Holub for Bete Noir on 14 October 1988. Then, his lengthy, almost tortuous lines had seemed nervous and clumsy when compared with Holub's brevity and wit. But his star had already started it's rise, winning the National Book Critic's Circle Award for **Flesh and Blood** (1987), and Williams has become one of the most highly-regarded poets in the U.S. Born in 1936, he has divided most of the last few decades between living in Paris and teaching at George Mason University in Virginia, though he has now moved to Princeton; his personal links are with mid-western writers and with the Confessionals, having had close friendships with both James Wright and Ann Sexton.His stylistic roots are with Whitman and Carlos Williams, his hallmarks emotional intensity and unremitting observation of neglected places and lives.

The evening's reading included a number of poems from his latest collection, **The Vigil**, a fine sampler of his style and concerns: the provisional nature of love and human relations, whether with parent, child or lover, the grief of the flesh and the grief of the moment," these transfigurations even of anguish that hold us (The Neighbour). Perhaps success has mellowed the previously lacerating sentiment and nervy hold on the reader that his work achieved in the early 1980s, but Williams remains a great witness to the mixed motives of consciousness, the times in general: regret, bitterness, compassion are there in abundance. Despite lacking variety and humour - Williams prefaced one poem by saying to the audience, "you can laugh if you want to," but few did - these poems contain many of the features and reasons that make people still value the art, and the chance to see poets in the flesh. His long, breathy line, driving onto the next, register the pungency and shabbiness of modern American life, and are his most authentic. He's capable of descents into bathos ("let me cling to your brainstem") and the occasional workshop exercise such as Villanelle of the Suicide's Mother, insisting after the reading that rhyme was not Un-American. The **Vigils**, however, is still a high-power read, full of energy and human interest.

Like C.K Williams, Stephen Dobyns originates from New Jersey (William Carlos Williams territory) and his poems appear in many of the same magazines, such as **American Poetry Review**, **Paris Review** and **Antaeus**. Again like CKW, he has his niche in the Creative Writing industry at American colleges, but there the similarities end. He is usually described as a storyteller, having produced 8 poetry volumes and 17, mostly Crime, novels; but in fact his work is only indirectly anecdotal, full of rhetorical questions and offbeat Americana. A level of philosophical complexity, and linguistic plain fare, informs the statement: "I am surrounded by unpleasant information / against which I set a mountain of distraction" (The World as Textbook). The tone of his poems tends to be matter-of-fact, lacking any sense of rapture, piling up details like a reporter; he appears not to bother with compression, and some poems meander for two or three pages when they may have been more memorable over one page. Dobyns has his admirers, for his verse and prose, and when he hits the elegiac note just right and in tune with American past culture - superbly in 'Thelonious Monk' and 'Lil'Darlin' - the result is moving. Being born in 1941, Dobyns is now inhabiting the position where there is more to look back on than to look forward to, and this collection particularly trawls through the decades for "my friends who died young...../ Look, our memories are stuffed with such stories" (Winter Nights). There are poems in Common Carnage that one wants to photocopy and send to friends, but the indirection of his methods, clogging naratives with questions, make the book less powerful than it may have been. There's a lot apparently happening in the poems, but not much registers; though Dobyns work is In the American Grain, it's likely to leave British readers lukewarm. "Is anxiety / a defense or a philosophy? Can one exist / in acts of self-negation?" (Who is Mistaken?) Who cares?

John Hartley Williams came to some prominence during the 1980s vogue for postmodernist 'play' with narrative (which seemsalmost as dead now as Martianism), winning the 1983 Arvon Prize and publishing **Bright River Yonder** in 1987, " a baroque Wild West poetry adventure". His combination of elements derived from European Surrealism and American Modernism

241

gained some influential admirers, notably his editor Neil Astley, the critics Michael Hulse, David Kennedy and David Morley, and, for one book at least, Sean O' Brien. The introduction to **The New Poetry** (1983) praised his fiction-making, his "questioning of ideas about poetic authority, sincerity and authenticity," indeed his "Postcognitive Questions: which of my selves is... "They relished his "fiction by ellipsis", thematic unity emerging out of disparate voices. But these semi-professional poetry chewers were chomping increasingly on sawdust; like many another, Hartley Williams followed up an initial success with books more self indulgent, and duller, than the last. The occasional lyric interlude in Cornerless People, if tin-eared, redeemed that book; several of these are reprinted in this current much fatter volume, either as a tribute to intertextuality or to sleepy editing. Playtime for professors - Hartley Williams teaches at the Free University of Berlin - becomes hard work for the pleasure seeking reader.

Canada turns out to be not a country but a quote from the French Surrealist Benjamin Peret; or, as the blurb puts it, Canada is "a country of the mind, where whatever mania comes to mind becomes it's own reality". What this means on the page is a lot of flattish statement, in-jokes, sexual fantasy, and word-scattering: imagine e.e. cummings mixed with a dash of Charles Olson and Surrealist quotes; oh, and some diluted Ian Duhigisms, with voices, literary schizophrenia, an ill- digested mix. Reviewing is nororiously subjective but only a poetry-chewer without taste buds could masticate this book for long. The reader is left rather like a subscriber to Satellite TV, desperately flicking through 127 channels for something decent to watch. Yet **Canada** was shortlisted for the 1997 T.S Eliot Prize, and was a Poetry Book Society Choice, so Hartley Williams still has friends in the right places. Does he have many readers? The decision .... is yours.

Jules Smith